-3

MW00466791

The Public Library of Cincinnati
and Hamilton County

DISCARD

262

THE COMPLETE GUIDE TO MINIATURE DACHSHUNDS

David Anderson

Copyright © 2018 David Anderson
All rights reserved.

TABLE OF CONTENTS

Introduction ... 6

CHAPTER 1
What is a Miniature Dachshund? ... 8
History of the Miniature Dachshund ... 8
Physical Characteristics ... 11
Behavioral Characteristics ... 12
Is a Miniature Dachshund the Right Fit for You? ... 14

CHAPTER 2
Choosing a Miniature Dachshund ... 16
Buying vs. Adopting ... 16
How to Find a Reputable Breeder ... 20
Researching Breeders ... 21
Health Tests and Certifications ... 22
Health Guarantees ... 22
Choosing Your Pick of the Litter ... 23
Tips for Adopting a Miniature Dachshund ... 24

CHAPTER 3
Preparing Your Home for Your Miniature Dachshund ... 26
Getting Your Children and Pets Ready ... 26
Dangerous Things a Dog Might Eat ... 29
Other Household Dangers ... 30
Preparing an Outdoor Space ... 33

CHAPTER 4
Bringing Home Your New Dog ... 34
Having a Plan ... 34
The Ride Home ... 34

The First Day **36**
Puppy's First Veterinarian Visit. **38**
Puppy Training Classes **40**
Getting Supplies Ready **41**
Cost Breakdown for the First Year **42**

CHAPTER 5

Being a Puppy Parent **44**
Standing by Your Expectations. **44**
How to Crate Train **45**
Chewing. **46**
Your Noisy Puppy. **47**
Digging. **48**
Separation Anxiety **49**
Running Away **50**
Bedtime **50**
Leaving Your Dog Home Alone. **51**

CHAPTER 6

Housetraining **52**
Different Options for Potty Training **52**
The First Few Weeks **53**
Rewarding Positive Behavior. **55**
Crate Training, Pens, and Doggy Doors **56**
Housetraining Adult Dogs. **57**

CHAPTER 7

Socialization **58**
The Benefits of Socialization **59**
Socialization with Other Dogs **60**
Socializing with Other Pets **61**
Socializing with Humans. **62**
Introducing Your Dog to Your Children **63**

CHAPTER 8

Miniature Dachshunds and Other Pets **64**
Introducing Your New Puppy. **64**

Pack Mentality **67**
Small Breed Psychology **68**
Fighting Between Your Dogs **69**
Raising Multiple Puppies from the Same Litter **70**
What If My Pets Don't Get Along? **71**

CHAPTER 9
Training Your Miniature Dachshund **72**
Setting Clear Expectations **72**
A Primer on Operant Conditioning **74**
Primary Reinforcement **76**
Secondary Reinforcement **77**
Dangers of Punishment **78**
Professional Dog Training **79**
Owner Behavior **80**

CHAPTER 10
Basic Commands **82**
Benefits of Obedience Training **82**
Basic Commands **85**
Advanced Commands **88**

CHAPTER 11
Dealing With Unwanted Behaviors **90**
What is Bad Behavior? **90**
Finding the Root of the Problem **91**
Bad Behavior Prevention **92**
How to Correct Your Dog **93**
Fixing Bad Habits **94**
When to Seek Help **95**

CHAPTER 12
Traveling with Miniature Dachshunds **96**
Dog Carriers and Restraints **96**
Getting Your Dog Ready for Rides **97**
Flying With Your Miniature Dachshund **98**
Hotel Stays **99**

Kennels and Dog Sitters **99**
Tips and Tricks for Traveling with Your Dog **100**

CHAPTER 13

Nutrition **102**
The Importance of a Good Diet **102**
Essential Nutrients for Miniature Dachshunds **103**
Different Types of Dog Foods **104**
Homemade Dog Foods **105**
Feeding Your Dog People Food **106**
Weight Management **106**

CHAPTER 14

Grooming your Miniature Dachshund **108**
Coat Care **108**
Bathing **109**
Trimming Nails **110**
Brushing Your Dog's Teeth **111**
Cleaning the Eyes and Ears **112**
Professional Grooming **112**

CHAPTER 15

Basic Healthcare **114**
Visiting the Veterinarian **114**
Fleas and Ticks **116**
Worms **117**
Supplements and Holistic Healthcare **117**
Vaccinations **118**
Pet Insurance **119**

CHAPTER 16

Advanced Miniature Dachshund Health **120**
Common Genetic Ailments in Miniature Dachshunds **120**
Health Risks in Small Dogs **122**
Illness and Injury Prevention **124**

CHAPTER 17
Life with an Aging Miniature Dachshund 126
Basics of Senior Dog Care 126
Grooming 128
Nutrition 130
Exercise 131
Mental Exercise 131
Senior Health 132
When It's Time To Say Goodbye 133

Introduction

A Miniature Dachshund is all of the fun of a standard-sized Dachshund, just in a smaller package. Originally bred as hunting dogs, these dogs are both physically and mentally strong. They were valued for their fearlessness as much as their strong digging skills and prey drive. These dogs were able to dig themselves into a burrow in order to catch and kill their prey.

Today, this breed has made the transition from fierce hunter to loyal family pet. They are highly protective of the people who love them and are great with children. Miniature Dachshunds will forget their size if they think their people are in danger, like a little watchdog. They may be small, but they have big voices and they'll be sure to let you know if something's up.

These dogs have a goofy personality to match their goofy appearance. With tiny legs and a long body, they'll be sure to attract a lot of attention on walks. The long ears and big feet on these sausage dogs complete their adorable look. Not only do they look a little silly, but they act the part as well. Miniature Dachshunds are a constant source of entertainment for their owners.

This book will cover everything you need to know about raising a Miniature Dachshund. From choosing a new puppy to senior dog care, this book touches on it all. Whether you're planning on bringing home a new Miniature Dachshund or you're looking for some tips to help you care for your dog, this book can help you figure out what you need to do.

We begin with a description of the breed, showing you both physical and behavioral characteristics. You'll find out why your dog loves to dig holes in the backyard and why it's prone to bark at the doorbell. You'll know the different possible appearances of this breed and which kind suits your home and lifestyle.

Next, we'll cover everything you need to know about picking out a new dog. Whether you're adopting or buying from a breeder, there are tips to help you every step of the way. You'll learn how to find a good breeder, which questions to ask, and how to pick out a healthy, happy pup. There's so much to know before you even bring your dog home, and this part of the book will help you on your way.

After you know how to pick out a good Miniature Dachshund, the next few chapters give a detailed look into preparing your home and family for a new dog. From preparing your home, to educating your children and pets on how to behave with a new puppy in the house, you'll be able to form your own checklist for things to do before bringing your puppy home. This part of the book includes lists of needed supplies, costs, and hidden dangers in your home.

Next, you'll discover what you should expect during the first few months with your new dog. This is a big transition period for everyone involved, and a bit of preparation can make things run much more smoothly. You will learn how to housetrain your new pup, how to socialize your dog with people and other animals, and how to make your new dog feel comfortable in your home.

Then, once your dog is comfortable in its new home, it's time to begin training. This part of the book covers the psychology of dog training, offering a little insight into how dogs think. The next chapter gives basic instructions about how to teach your dog to perform necessary commands. Then, for an added challenge, there are a few bonus commands that can keep your dog's mind sharp.

The next section covers daily life with your dog. You'll learn the best ways to travel with your new companion. Then, we'll examine everything you need to know about a Miniature Dachshund's nutritional and exercise needs. Plus, you'll learn about how good grooming habits can extend the life and happiness of your dog.

Finally, the book will go over basic healthcare, health conditions that are prevalent in Mini Dachshunds, and the senior stage of your dog's life. After reading this section, you'll know all the signs and symptoms to look out for as the prime advocate in your dog's healthcare.

There is a lot that goes into raising a Miniature Dachshund, but the time and effort it takes to do things right is worth it. In the end, you'll find that your new puppy will blossom into a well-behaved, happy, and healthy adult. The greatest gift that an owner can give to a Miniature Dachshund is a willingness and commitment to making its life the best that it can be.

CHAPTER 1
What is a Miniature Dachshund?

A Miniature Dachshund is a Dachshund that is specifically bred to be smaller than the Standard Dachshund. Also commonly referred to as a "wiener dog", this breed is distinguished by its long body and short legs. While the Dachshund is recognized by all dog breeding organizations, the Miniature Dachshund isn't formally recognized. However, like the Toy Poodle, this breed has become so commonplace that most dog enthusiasts know about it.

With dogs, any variations on the standard size tend to exhibit different physical and behavioral traits. But, for the most part, Miniature Dachshunds share many qualities with their standard-sized ancestors. So in order to know more about the miniature version of this breed, it helps to know about the Standard Dachshund.

History of the Miniature Dachshund

Dachshunds can be traced all the way back to 15th century Germany. These dogs had a strong prey drive, making them well-suited for hunting badgers, foxes, and even wild boars. Over the next few centuries, their bodies became even shorter and longer, making them the perfect size for wiggling into burrows to hunt. These dogs are unique because they will hunt animals both above and below the earth. As opposed to other breeds of hunting dogs, Dachshunds were used for killing their prey as well as tracking it.

Certain traits made Dachshunds succeed as hunters. Their strong but small bodies made it possible to enter a burrow to fight their prey to the death. They have a loud, deep bark that allowed hunters to follow them. Large paws helped them excel at digging into the burrows. And their headstrong behavior made them fearless in dangerous situations.

Over the last few centuries, the breed has gone from a fierce hunter to a household pet. Like many other breeds, being a favorite in a royal court was a sure-fire way to spread its popularity. They transitioned out of being working dogs and were bred to be more docile. Still, they kept their fiery personalities, making them fun dogs to have around.

The breed showed a decline in popularity in the United States around the time of World War I, due to the breed being a German export. However, the breed gained more traction in the following decades. Today, the Standard Dachshund is one of the most widely recognized dogs in the world.

At the end of the 19th century, German hunters found that the Standard Dachshund was occasionally too large to fit into the small burrows of hares. To fix this problem, the smallest of the litter was typically chosen for the small jobs. Finding that the littlest of the Dachshunds were useful, their owners bred them with other toy-sized dogs or selectively bred them amongst other small Dachshunds. Eventually, the Miniature Dachshund was created. Through selective breeding, these dogs kept the same tough spirit as the standard-sized dogs, but with a smaller stature.

Today, Miniature Dachshunds are favored by owners who love how cute and petite these dogs are. Their goofy, low-to-the-ground stature is even more adorable in a smaller size. This breed has a ton of attitude packed into a tiny body.

Photo Courtesy of
Christine Clements
Wire Hair

*Photo Courtesy of
Tina Green
Long Haired*

Physical Characteristics

While the Standard Dachshund can weigh up to thirty pounds as an adult, the Miniature Dachshund typically will never get larger than eleven pounds. Dachshunds that weigh anywhere between eleven and sixteen pounds as an adult are referred to as "tweenies" because they are in between Miniature and Standard size. Of course, these ranges reflect the dogs' size at a healthy weight.

Though they're not often used for hunting these days, the Miniature Dachshund still has the body for burrowing and hunting. This breed is easily recognized by its longer-than-average body and shorter-than-average legs. They have large paddle-like paws and a deep chest. Their small, pointed faces are flanked with long, floppy ears. Their strong, pointed tails made the perfect handle for their handlers to pull them out of holes (though tail-pulling might not be appreciated by pet Dachshunds).

Miniature Dachshunds can have three different coat types: smooth, wirehaired, and longhaired. Perhaps the most common coat is the smooth coat. This coat is short and glossy. Red and cream coats are fairly common with the smooth type. Some smooth coated Miniature Dachshunds have two colors to their coat. These include combinations of black, dark brown, grey, tan, or red. Even rarer are the dapple coats, which have a light and dark merle pattern. Dappled Miniature Dachshunds may even have blue eyes. Because their fur is so short, grooming them is fairly simple. Brushing may help you cut down on shedding in the home, but this type isn't prone to matting like the longer haired types.

Because they don't have a lot of fur to keep them warm, the smooth coated Mini Dachshunds require clothing to keep them warm in extreme cold. If you live in a place that experiences freezing temperatures make sure your Mini Dachshund has a sweater or jacket to keep it warm. These dogs do not like the cold and the rain, making it hard for you to convince your dog to go outside to use the bathroom in inclement weather.

The wirehaired type also has a short coat, but with a few differences. They have short, thick hair on top, but underneath the top coat is a soft undercoat. This soft undercoat gives the appearance of a beard, bushy eyebrows, and fluffier ears. The same colors found in the smooth coated Miniature Dachshund are common for the wirehaired Dachshund. However, the "wild boar" markings (black and red) are most common. This coat type requires regular brushing to keep the undercoat from becoming matted.

Finally, the longhaired Miniature Dachshund has a longer, wavier coat than the other types. Their long fur should be soft and smooth, with just a hint of a wavy texture. While they can come in the same colors as the other coat types, lighter colors are typically more common. With this coat type, frequent brushing is a necessity because the long fur can become tangled and matted easily.

When it comes to eye colors, this breed has a wide range, depending on the coat color. Generally, the lighter the coat, the lighter the eye color. Red and black coated Mini Dachshunds typically have dark brown eyes, while fawn or merle pups may have blue, green, hazel, or light brown eyes. It's even possible for some dogs to have two different colored eyes.

While Mini Dachshunds have muscular, compact bodies, they should never look chunky or overweight. This breed can easily become obese, wreaking havoc on their health. Their broad chest should taper off throughout their body, tucking in at the waistline. When looking at the Mini Dachshund from above, there should be a clear curve from shoulders to hips, never a straight line. A chubby dog may look cute, but any extra weight can put a lot of stress on a dog's body.

Behavioral Characteristics

To understand a Miniature Dachshund's behavior, it helps to understand their history and what they were originally bred for. Miniature Dachshunds are lively, energetic dogs that sometimes have a mind of their own. Dachshund owners love the big confidence that comes from such a tiny dog. These dogs know that they are great and want you to know it, too.

This breed should never be shy or timid. Any sign of shyness in this bold dog may point to underlying psychological or breeding issues. They hold their tiny heads high and are independent. Sometimes shyness is found in Miniature Dachshunds, but this is more indicative of poor breeding or socialization than it is size-related. Even the tiniest of the Miniature Dachshunds should have that trademark confidence.

Miniature Dachshunds are lively dogs that love to play. Their little legs won't require as long of a walk as other active dogs, so they can get a lot of their exercise just from playing with their owners. They may not be big enough to catch a Frisbee, but they love chasing after toys. Give this breed plenty of toys to play with to keep them entertained. Keep in mind that Mini Dachshunds like to give chase, so don't be surprised when you see them running after kids or other pets. Exercise is important for this breed because of their tendency to gain weight, so make sure they get plenty of exercise during the day. One walk and a few chances to play every day should be sufficient.

Just because this breed is independent doesn't mean that they don't want to be cuddled. These dogs will form a close bond with their owners and want to protect them from danger. They might not be fond of strangers at first, but once they have some time to warm up to them, they can be very friendly. Don't be surprised if your Mini Dachshund barks when people come to the door. They can be taught not to do that, but barking is what will likely come as their first instinct.

Having a moderately independent dog is a great thing. While it's fun to have your dog follow you around like a shadow, it can be hard to leave your dog home alone if it has a hard time without you. Dachshunds offer the best of both worlds—they like to be around their people, but they won't suffer if they have to be alone for a few hours. This makes them a good pet if you work during the day.

While these dogs are quite intelligent, they are also stubborn, making training a challenge. With time, they will learn to obey your commands, but it will take lots of practice. This breed will make up their own rules if you let them, so obedience training is a must. They are fairly sensitive to human reactions, so they'll be able to pick up human cues telling them what is and what isn't acceptable behavior. Housetraining and obedience training will take a little extra work with Miniature Dachshunds, but once they understand that they have a job to do, they'll be able to learn your commands with ease.

Smooth Hair

Overall, this is a lively breed with a stubborn streak. They're brave pups that love to play. Mini Dachshunds love owners that will give them love and affection, plus plenty of exercise. They may be difficult to train at times, but they're truly intelligent dogs that like to test their owners. With so much personality in such a little dog, it's easy to see why Miniature Dachshunds are a favorite of dog owners.

Is a Miniature Dachshund the Right Fit for You?

Some dog breeds are better suited to certain owners than others. Before bringing any new dog home, a prospective owner needs to have an honest look at their resources and personality before making this major commitment. When thinking about your ability to care for a dog, consider your time, energy, home environment, family, pets, and monetary resources. If all of those things align with the Miniature Dachshund's needs, then it will make a lovely addition to your home. Adding a dog to an ill-equipped household isn't fair to the dog or the owner.

The type of home you live in isn't a major issue for these dogs because they are so small and aren't excessively energetic. They make fine apartment pets as long as they have the opportunity to go outside a few times a day. Large homes are no problem either, as long as they aren't kept in a yard all day. They can get cold fairly easily, so being exposed to the elements for a long period of time can take a toll on their health. Plus, they'll want to spend time with their owners whenever possible.

Next, look at how much time your household can reasonably devote to your dog. Mini Dachshunds aren't particularly needy, but they shouldn't be left alone for long periods of time. For example, they can probably spend the day at home while you're at work, but they'll need some attention over the lunch hour. However, if your schedule doesn't allow you to spend several hours each day with your dog, then maybe this isn't the right breed for you.

Finally, consider how much energy you have to put into caring for your dog. While they don't need a ton of your physical energy to keep them healthy, it takes a lot of mental energy to deal with a stubborn animal. If you're a calm, patient person who is willing to do whatever you can to train your dog, then this breed is a good fit for you. On the other hand, if you become frustrated easily and give up when things become challenging, this breed will likely exhaust your patience. Be prepared to spend a lot of time working on the same commands until your dog decides it wants to learn.

If you find that you have all of the qualities needed to become the loving owner of a Miniature Dachshund, then you can begin to research places to find your new pup. If you find that you come up short in a few areas of Miniature Dachshund care, that doesn't mean that you'll never be fit to raise this breed. But it will save everyone stress in the long run if you're completely prepared to take on the challenge of raising a Miniature Dachshund.

These tiny sausage dogs are so much fun to be around. They have so much personality and they just want a good owner to love. Since they come in so many different colors and coat types, there's a Mini Dachshund for everyone. Once you take yours home, you'll instantly fall in love with its silly personality and peppy disposition. They can be a challenge at times, but having them around is a real reward.

CHAPTER 2
Choosing a Miniature Dachshund

"Be sure to see what the dam and sire look and act like. If you like the way the parents look and act chances are you will be happy with your new puppy."

Reba Mandrell
www.heartlanddachshunds.com

Now that you know you're ready for a Miniature Dachshund, it's time to figure out the best place to find your dog. There are a lot of things to consider before finding a place to buy or adopt a Miniature Dachshund. No matter where you get your dog, make sure it comes from a place where it received proper care and there are knowledgeable people that can answer your questions about the breed.

Buying vs. Adopting

There are two sources to consider when looking for a dog. There are advantages and disadvantages to both buying and adopting, so you'll need to research and think about what you're looking for in a dog.

First of all, adopting a dog just feels good. You're taking an abandoned dog into your loving home. Dogs in shelters don't always get a lot of one-on-one time with people, and some are even euthanized if the shelter cannot care for them. Often times, senior dogs are not adopted because prospective owners know that they won't have a lot of time with them before they die. However, you may find that a senior dog is more relaxed, which makes them better suited for some homes.

Rescue Miniature Dachshunds will also come with a health care history from their previous owners, or just because they lived in the shelter in the first place. When you're getting a dog from a shelter, you get a lot more than just the dog. They'll likely be up to date on all of their vaccinations, be spayed or neutered, and possibly even micro chipped.

Adoption gives a good dog a new home, while saving you money up front. Because the shelter's top priority is finding good homes for their dogs, the re-homing fee is a lot less than a purchase price. In fact, you may even spend less than the sticker price for vaccinations, spaying/ neutering procedures, and micro chipping. For someone trying to save

18

money to afford the costs associated with dog ownership, adoption is a great deal. Buying from good breeders can be very expensive, because you are paying for their expertise and their hard work in taking care of the mother and puppies.

There are numerous benefits to adopting that many people don't realize. In a lot of cases, adopted dogs have spent time in a loving home. They had a previous owner that took the time to housetrain, obedience train, and socialize them with people or animals. When you get a previously owned dog, a lot of the hard work has already been taken care of. Especially for this breed, finding a dog that's already mastered basic training skills is a huge plus. If they were well trained, then it's possible that their temperament will allow for more advanced training.

But there are also disadvantages that need to be considered. When you adopt a dog from a shelter, you don't always know its back story. A lot of times, pets are given up because the owners couldn't take care of a dog with their current life circumstances. Other times, it's because there was a conflict with the dog. This isn't necessarily the dog's fault in every scenario. Sometimes, owners don't take the time to socialize or train their dogs, then decide that they have to give their dog away because it's using the house as a bathroom. Sometimes, owners bring in new pets without considering how they'll interact with other pets. It is possible to have a dog that does not get along with other animals or children. In this instance, you might not want to choose a dog that has a history of being aggressive towards children if you have a new baby. But

an animal shelter should have a decent idea whether their animals have problems with others.

If you're set on finding a Miniature Dachshund puppy, you might not be able to find one for quite some time. They're not a relatively common breed, so you'll probably have to wait until the right one is available. Everyone wants the cute Mini Dachshund puppy, so the adults get left behind. You might also encounter the fact that there are Miniature Dachshunds available for adoption, but they're mixed with different breeds. If you aren't picky about what kind of Miniature Dachshund you get, then adopting is a great option.

Many people don't realize that an animal shelter doesn't just hand out dogs to anyone. Because they care about the future of their animals, many shelters make prospective owners fill out questionnaires or adoption applications to ensure that they are capable of handling a specific breed. You may also find that a volunteer will visit your home before they release a Miniature Dachshund to you. In the end, this is in everyone's best interests and shouldn't be a big deal if you've prepared your home for a pet. This breed probably won't require a big backyard, but someone might want to make sure that your home is safe for a dog. For Miniature Dachshunds, this means that they need a small space to be able to play and somewhere they can go to the bathroom. If you live in an apartment, you will need to ensure they cannot access a balcony.

If you aren't sure where to start looking for a Mini Dachshund to adopt, the Internet is full of useful resources. There are websites that allow prospective owners to search for dogs by breed, sex, and age in your area. Depending on how badly you want to adopt the right dog, you can even search different parts of the country. If transportation is an issue, there are rescues so eager to re-home their dogs that they will find volunteers to bring their dogs to new owners.

The adoption process can be long and arduous, but once you have your new Mini Dachshund in your home, you'll realize how much it was worth it. While it might seem intrusive to have someone ask you questions about your life and visit your home, it's for the health and happiness of both you and your new pet. It may take some extra time and effort to find the right Miniature Dachshund, but it's a great feeling to give a deserving pup a forever home.

On the other hand, you don't always know what you're getting with an adopted dog. This uncertainty can make some owners nervous. If you have a particular dog in mind, it may take a while for the right Miniature Dachshund to enter a shelter and become available for adoption. Dogs that come from a reputable breeder are generally more predictable than adopted dogs because they should come from good parents and haven't had the chance to learn unwanted behaviors yet. Buying a Miniature

Photo Courtesy of
Tina Green

Dachshund is a good choice if you know exactly what you want in a dog and you have the funds to pay for it.

When you purchase a Miniature Dachshund from a breeder, you're buying a fairly uniform product. The health and temperament of a pup can generally be traced back to its parents. With a new puppy, you're so-cializing and training the dog from the very beginning of its life. You'll know that your dog came from good stock and the breeder will have the records to back up its pedigree. For many owners, buying is preferred because it allows one to be the sole caregiver for an animal.

When thinking about buying versus adopting a Mini Dachshund, think about how much time, energy, and money you have to spend on a new dog. Also imagine the perfect Mini Dachshund. If there's something very specific you want in the dog, you may opt to shop around with dif-ferent breeders to find it. Otherwise, you may decide that you want to give a shelter dog a new home. There is no right or wrong answer when it comes to the question of where to get your new dog. Ultimately, own-ers must choose what is best for their home.

How to Find a Reputable Breeder

Good dog breeders know what they're doing and are committed to delivering good work. Breeding should not be done by amateurs because it takes an understanding of genetics and breed traits to get it right. Both parents must be healthy and even-tempered dogs. For example, a tim-id parent can lead to a timid puppy. Anyone can find two Dachshunds to reproduce, but that doesn't necessarily mean the puppies will have the desirable traits found in a well-bred dog.

If your Miniature Dachshund is not properly bred, this can result in genetic diseases. Genetic ailments can be passed down from generation to generation. Backyard breeders may think that they're producing new and exciting puppies, but they very well may be passing down unwant-ed traits. If a breeder tries to breed Miniature Dachshunds smaller than they should be, the pups could suffer from developmental issues. Skilled breeders will work with Miniature Dachshunds because they're passion-ate about the breed, not because they're trying to get rich. Find someone who has been in the Mini Dachshund business for a long time, not some-one who follows fads.

Once you find a few breeders, ask if you can visit their homes. They should be happy to show you their business. When you're there, make sure the dogs are well cared for. They should have a clean living space, clean water, and plenty of toys to play with. A breeder with something to hide or a dirty living space for the dogs may not have the same pride in their work as a good breeder.

Before you buy your new dog, you should have a few conversations with the breeder. They should be available to you for any questions that you may have. Good breeders want their pups to go to good homes, so don't be surprised if they ask you a lot of questions in return. There should be an open line of communication between the two of you as you go through the purchasing process. If your breeder can't answer your questions, or doesn't allow you to see their operations, that should be a warning sign.

Researching Breeders

Once you know what a good breeder looks like, you're ready to start your research. Start by compiling a list of Miniature Dachshund breeders in your area. You can do an Internet search, talk to local vets, or ask around to other Miniature Dachshund owners.

An easy place to start your research is on the web. Most breeders have websites or pages on social media, dedicated to their Miniature Dachshunds. Once you find their place on the web, there are a few things you want to look for.

First, make sure that they aren't breeding a bunch of different types of dogs. Someone who breeds both Mini Dachshunds and Labradoodles is probably in the business to make money off of trendy breeds. Next, look for their credentials. If someone does quality work, they probably show their dogs in competition. Check to see if they have completed any courses or won any awards for their dogs. Finally, look for good feedback. A reputable breeder is proud of their work and will show lots of pictures of their operations. They will answer customer questions quickly and thoroughly. You may find that they are happy to get updates from people who have purchased dogs from them.

Once you've narrowed your search, you might want to call around to the different breeders and ask if you can pay them a visit. They should be willing to set up a time for you to come by. This is a great time to have a chat with the breeder and ask them everything you want to know about their work. You may ask them about their prices, health clearances, and other policies relating to their dogs.

The breeder may even let you meet the parents. These dogs should be friendly and meet the description found in the previous chapter. There shouldn't be any sign of shyness nor aggression in these dogs.

Look around where the dogs are kept and make sure that the area is clean and comfortable for the dogs.

If you still can't decide between breeders after visiting their homes, ask them for client references. It helps to know that another Mini Dachshund owner is pleased with their puppy. Plus, the fact that a breeder is willing to put you in contact with their clients is a good sign in itself.

Health Tests and Certifications

Because it's so easy for diseases to be passed down from one generation to another, health tests and health clearances give the owner some assurance that their new puppy won't become ill later in life. Good breeders will have health clearances for the dogs that they use to breed and be willing to show them to a client at any time.

Because some health problems don't show up until a Mini Dachshund is two to three years old, a breeder shouldn't use young dogs for breeding. Once the dogs reach adulthood, most genetic diseases will be detectable.

In Miniature Dachshunds, there are some diseases that are more common than others. Your breeder should have clearances for eye disease. This breed is prone to retinal dystrophy that causes gradual blindness. You also want to make sure that the parents have healthy spines because disc disease can leave a Dachshund paralyzed if it isn't treated.

Health Guarantees

Your breeder will probably insist that you take your new puppy to the vet to be checked out shortly after purchasing it. Before the puppies can be separated from their mother, they will visit the vet to get a checkup and receive their first vaccinations. Part of the reason this is done is because the breeder wants to ensure the puppies are healthy before letting customers take them home. But the second vet visit is necessary to protect the breeder, too. If one of their dogs becomes ill later in life, they'll need to know if it was their fault. If their puppies develop genetic diseases, then the breeder will want to know in order to ensure it doesn't happen again.

If the breeder was at fault, they may want to provide the owner with a partial discount, or an offer to cover some of the medical expenses. Health guarantees vary from breeder to breeder, so make sure you read the contract thoroughly before signing.

Choosing Your Pick of the Litter

When it's finally time to pick out your puppy, talk to the breeder about coming to visit the new puppies. While it may seem easier to look at a picture and choose the cutest one, there is more to consider than just appearance.

Of course, the Mini Dachshund's appearance is something to keep in mind. If you have your heart set on a dog with a smooth, red coat, then you should choose one with those features. When looking at a pup, watch it walk around and note any abnormalities in its movements. A good breeder will probably have already noticed any problems, but it's good to double check.

The reason you want to pick a puppy out in person is because there are some personalities that are more desirable than others. With dogs, you're looking for one that doesn't have too strong of a personality on either end of the spectrum. If there's one puppy that's particularly dominant and pushes the others around, it might grow up to be especially

Photo Courtesy of
Pauline Goring

stubborn. On the other hand, you don't want the puppy that's extremely shy and doesn't warm up to humans. Mini Dachshunds should never be timid. All puppies might be a little wary around a stranger at first, but they should warm up to people quickly.

Look for a dog that's content playing with the others and will allow you to pet it, but is also fine doing its own thing. With the right training, this dog will grow up to be a confident, friendly Miniature Dachshund. After about eight weeks from its birthday, it's time to take your new dog home. Puppies need to spend enough time with their mother and siblings, so the breeder should not be willing to send them home too early.

Tips for Adopting a Miniature Dachshund

When picking out a Miniature Dachshund from a shelter, some of the same tips apply for picking a puppy from a litter. You'll want to spend some time with the dog before bringing it into your home. Remember, if you find that the dog is not right for you after a few visits, then don't assume things will change once it comes home with you. While you may be eager to bring a cute Mini Dachshund into your home, make sure everything is perfect first.

The first time you meet the dog, don't come on too strong. Give it a second to sniff you out before petting it. Once the dog feels comfortable with you, ask the shelter if you can take it on a walk or spend some time playing with it. Here, you can really start to see its personality come forward. After a bit of play time, you'll start to be able to tell if it is shy, aggressive, stubborn, or mild-mannered.

It's also important to have a discussion with the shelter workers about the dog's behavior. Hopefully, the previous owner will have given them information about the dog. If you already have other pets, ask them how the Mini Dachshund is around other animals. If you have children, or plan to in the near future, make sure the dog wasn't sent to the shelter for attacking a child. If the dog is not a good fit for your home due to its past, then it might not be the one.

There is always a chance that a good owner can coax a nervous dog out of its shell. However, this is best to try if you live by yourself. Mini Dachshunds are likely to latch onto one person, so a pup with behavioral issues may have problems with other people or pets. Dogs that get annoyed by other animals or children aren't necessarily bad dogs, and they need homes, too.

After meeting with the dog a few times, ask the shelter if you can have it visit your home. This will help you gauge how it will do when you bring it home for good. This allows you to be in a no-pressure scenario in case something doesn't work out. You don't want to have to pay the fees just to find out that you can't keep the dog.

Adopting a Miniature Dachshund is an extremely rewarding experience. But, it's only rewarding if everyone involved is happy. Adoption is a great option for owners who don't need the perfect purebred or would rather not spend hundreds of dollars buying a puppy. It's also great for those who want a jumpstart on training and socializing. Before buying a dog, consider looking for a dog that needs a good home. It can make a huge difference in a Dachshund's life.

Once you find your perfect Miniature Dachshund, the fun can begin. Finding the right dog takes a lot of work, but it will save you stress in the future if you can pick a dog that's off to a good start. When choosing a dog, think about the qualities you want in a Miniature Dachshund. Pick one that will fit in with your lifestyle and your home.

CHAPTER 3

Preparing Your Home for Your Miniature Dachshund

"Miniature Dachshunds can fit into almost any lifestyle. Whether you are in an apartment or on a farm, relaxed or active, have kids or single."

Brittney LaCosse
www.havendachs.weebly.com

Before you even bring your new Miniature Dachshund into your home, there is some work that needs to be done. It's much easier to prepare your home for your new dog before it arrives than it is to make adjustments while keeping an eye on your pup.

When preparing your home, look for anything that could be dangerous for your dog to get into and anything you don't want your dog to ruin. Dogs like to explore by picking things up and feeling them with their mouths. Puppies are especially curious and have yet to learn that some things are off limits for them to chew. As a precaution, keep valuable objects out of reach until they learn to keep the chewing to their toys.

Along with your physical possessions, you'll also want to consider the other members of your family. Perhaps you live with other people or animals that aren't used to being around dogs. In this instance, you'll need to do a little homework to ensure everyone will be happy and safe with a new dog in the house.

Getting Your Children and Pets Ready

Mini Dachshunds get along well with children once they have warmed up to them. Before bringing a dog home, it's good to talk with young children about how to treat dogs, especially if they don't have a lot of experience with canines.

Keep in mind, if your children are very young, they should never be allowed to spend time with the dog without adult supervision. This is for the safety of both your kids and the dog. Both young children and dogs can act unpredictably. If something goes wrong, there's a chance that the child or the dog could be hurt, physically and emotionally.

Photo Courtesy of
Lisa Korab

Show kids the proper way to pet a dog. Teach them to approach a dog slowly and carefully to gently pet its back. It's best to teach little ones to pet the back of the dog, and to stay away from the face. Little fingers can easily be bitten if they get too close to the face. You may have the gentlest Mini Dachshund in the world, but if it gets an accidental poke to the eye, it will probably have some sort of response. Also, if you're bringing home a puppy, it hasn't learned that it isn't supposed to nibble on people's fingers. A puppy typically won't bite too hard, but for small children, tiny teeth on their fingers can be painful and scary.

Because Miniature Dachshunds have such long bodies, they are more susceptible to spine damage than most dogs. If Mini Dachshunds are ever picked up, they need proper support. They need to be held with one arm supporting their bottom and the other on their chest. Also, because this dog is so small, rough play is more likely to cause injuries. Make sure that energetic children know that they need to be careful around such a tiny dog.

Miniature Dachshunds are brave, so your dog may be inclined to stand up for itself rather than run away from a stressful situation. For equally brave children, this may pose an issue when it turns into a standoff. For this reason, teach your children to respect your dog's space, and teach your dog to be gentle with kids as well.

For older children, having a dog is a great way to teach them about responsibility and caring for others. Kids can help out by making sure your Mini Dachshund has food and clean water. They can play with the dog and take it on walks. Also, all family members should have a hand in obedience training. That way, your dog will be comfortable taking commands from everyone. If you take a training course, bring your kids along. They'll learn a new skill and your dog will get plenty of practice at home.

Once you've picked out the perfect Miniature Dachshund, have your kids meet it before it comes home. Not only will it give you a way to gauge how your dog will act around them, but it gives the dog an opportunity to get to know its new family members. Give the dog a few moments to sniff them and check them out before they start petting the dog. This way, the Mini Dachshund is less likely to become frightened and stressed out.

Another reason to have your kids meet the dog first is because getting a new dog is a very exciting time. If your kids have already worked out their excitement before the dog comes home, that's one more thing your pup won't have to worry about. Mini Dachshunds get along with kids, but screaming children in a strange place is enough to make any dog nervous.

Finally, talk to your kids about your dog's body language. If a dog drops its head low to the ground or has its tail between its legs, this means that it is upset and it needs some space to relax. If a dog growls, this is a warning that it is stressed out and will snap at someone to protect itself. When a dog shows these warning signs, let your kids know that their dog needs space to calm down and they should stop whatever they are doing.

Getting a new dog is a wonderful moment in a child's life that they will remember forever. If you want the moment to be special for your dog, make sure it feels comfortable around young people. This will en-sure that your dog and your kids have a great relationship.

Dangerous Things a Dog Might Eat

For dogs, the best way to learn about their surroundings is by pick-ing up everything they can find in their mouth. If they happen to find something that they think is tasty, they have no problem eating it. Unfortunately, there are certain things in the home that are very dan-gerous for dogs to eat. Before bringing your dog home, it's a good idea to eliminate these things, or at least put them out of reach of your dog. Fortunately, because the Mini Dachshund is so tiny, just a high shelf or cabinet may be enough to keep dangerous things away.

There are two types of things your dog might try to eat. The first is people food. There are several foods that humans can eat with no issues that will cause illness in dogs. The second is inedible objects or plants that your dog might try to eat anyway. Both require immediate veteri-nary care if ingested.

Most owners know that chocolate is not good for dogs, but some may not know how dangerous it can really be. Because the Miniature Dachshund is such a small creature, just a small serving of a toxic sub-stance can cause serious illness. Symptoms include vomiting, seizures and shock, and if your dog doesn't receive care, it can die. Keep in mind that foods that contain chocolate are dangerous, too.

Speaking of sweets, even fake sugar is bad for dogs. Xylitol is a sugar substitute found in a lot of sugar free candies, gums, and baked goods. A few bites can cause vomiting and diarrhea. It's hard to know the ingre-dients in everything you eat, so resist the temptation to feed your dog a few nibbles of your snacks.

Grapes, raisins, onions, coffee, macadamia nuts, and avocados are seemingly harmless foods that just don't agree with a dog's body. If your dog eats any of these things, call your vet as soon as possible, because organ failure is likely. If you aren't sure whether your dog has ingested something dangerous, check for any symptoms like excessive thirst, changes in breathing, drowsiness, vomiting, diarrhea, or any other abnormalities.

Just to be safe, keep your houseplants out of reach of your dog. While some plants are safe for your dog to chew on, others, like lilies, can poison your dog. Hanging baskets are great for dog owners because they can enjoy their plants without worrying about their dogs taking a bite. Otherwise, keep plants on shelves and tables that are off limits to your dog.

Finally, never underestimate the strange things your dog will try to eat. Small objects, like coins and small toys, can be easily swallowed. If a dog eats an inedible object, it must be passed, whether it has been digested or not. This can be highly unpleasant for your dog. If an object cannot be passed, then your dog can wind up with an internal obstruction. A dog that doesn't eat or drink may be experiencing an obstruction. If not treated, this can be deadly. In most cases, surgery is needed to remove the object from the intestines. If there is something in your home that you'd rather not have your dog eat, place it in a drawer or on a high shelf. You don't want your dog to become ill, and the resulting vet bill could be astronomical.

Other Household Dangers

Before bringing your new puppy home, do a quick sweep of your house while thinking like a dog. What might your dog get into while you're not looking that can cause it harm? There are a few rooms in the house that have more hidden dangers than others.

The bathroom is a good place to start. Make sure there is no way your feisty pup can get into any of your hygiene products or cleaning chemicals. Keep belongings like toothpaste safely tucked into drawers. You might think your pup won't be able to reach the toilet to take a sip, but never underestimate the power of a determined Dachshund. It's safest just to keep the lid down.

Laundry rooms are also filled with things that should not be ingested. A stray sock or pair of underwear can become a choking hazard or an internal obstruction. Cleaning products may smell interesting to a dog, but the chemicals they contain can be very dangerous.

Finally, make sure there is nothing in the garage that your dog can get into. Products like pesticides, fertilizers, and rodent poisons can kill a small dog. While it's best to try to eliminate those products altogether, at the very least, make sure they are kept out of reach. If your Miniature

Dachshund manages to ingest something that toxic, it won't have much time before it needs to see a vet.

Your home may feel like a deathtrap for a dog, but if you take the right precautions and use a little common sense, you'll have no problem. Just like baby-proofing a home, you have to think about what a small dog can possibly get into. Dachshunds are determined animals—once they make up their minds to do something, they will. They are also smart and crafty, so you may need to utilize locks and gates to keep your dog safe.

Preparing an Indoor Space

Just like people like to have their own personal space every once in a while, dogs need to have a place of their own, too. For a new puppy, you'll want to section off a small area where it can hang out during the day. In this area, give it fresh water, a bed or crate, and possibly a potty pad if you're using them for the puppy stage. There are pens and gates at pet stores that are perfect for keeping your dog out of trouble.

If you don't plan on using a pen, consider gating off an area of your house for your Miniature Dachshund to spend time while it's in the pup-

Photo Courtesy of
Jim Braner

py stage. When housetraining, it's easier to keep an eye on it if it's not hiding all over the house. Give it a room or two to hang out in, but leave other rooms off limits during the day.

If you choose to crate train your dog, this can be a wonderful place for your Miniature Dachshund to sleep. When trained correctly, your dog will associate its crate with safety and comfort, so if it gets stressed out, it can spend time in there. Both metal and plastic crates are good options and can even help with housetraining.

Finally, make sure that it can access plenty of toys in its space. If left unsupervised, these dogs can get bored. A bored dog can become a destructive dog very quickly. Give your dog something to chew on, and it'll be much happier if it must be alone for a short amount of time.

Photo Courtesy of
Sarah Schwartz

Preparing an Outdoor Space

A backyard isn't a necessity for the well-being of a dog as small as your Miniature Dachshund. These dogs can live in apartments without any problems because they don't take up a lot of space.

If you live in a home without a yard, make sure you have at least one nearby location for your dog to get some exercise and use the bathroom. A dog park can be a nice place to socialize with other people and dogs, while giving your dog the freedom to stretch its legs. Before bringing your dog home, find a few places nearby for your dog to roam.

If you do have a yard, you'll want to make sure that it provides the safety that your dog needs. You probably won't have to worry about your Miniature Dachshund jumping over a fence, but you will have to worry about it wiggling underneath or through cracks. Miniature Dachshunds are great at digging, so if yours is known to burrow, you'll want to make sure it's not planning an escape. Routinely check the perimeter of your yard for exit points.

Also, consider making an outdoor shelter for your dog. Sometimes it's nice to let your dog enjoy the fresh air for a few hours. However, this breed doesn't do well in extreme heat or cool temperatures. If your dog is outside for a while, make sure it has somewhere to sit in the shade in the summer, and a warm shelter in the cooler months. This breed should not be kept as outdoor dogs all the time, but a few hours outside during the day is good for them.

Once your home is prepared, it's time to bring your new Miniature Dachshund home. It may seem stressful anticipating a new dog's needs, but it's good to be prepared so you can devote all of your time to playing with your new puppy. A prepared home makes for a seamless transition from old home to new.

CHAPTER 4
Bringing Home Your New Dog

After picking out your dog and preparing your household for its arrival, you're ready to bring your dog into your home. This is a big change of scene for a dog that may have only lived in one home its whole life. Luckily, your brave little Miniature Dachshund will become accustomed to your home in no time. This chapter is a quick guide to everything you need to know about the first few days of owning a new Miniature Dachshund.

Having a Plan

Chances are if you're reading this book, you're someone who wants to be prepared for everything. Good dog owners are willing to do a lot to make their dogs a little happier and healthier. By planning ahead, you'll get your Mini Dachshund off to a good start in life.

Dogs are susceptible to stress, which is not good for their bodies. While these animals don't have great memories, they can be conditioned into making connections between feelings of stress and your home.

Because there's so much going on already, there isn't really time to deal with a stressed-out puppy. With a nervous dog, you'll find that housetraining is difficult and socialization can be set back as well.

In order to combat the anxiety new owners and new dogs feel, it's best to have a plan. When you know which items to buy and how to introduce your dog to others, things will run much more smoothly. Of course, remember to be flexible when necessary, because all dogs are different. You may find that your Mini Dachshund is taking a little longer to become housetrained, and that's okay. But, if you know what you're doing, you'll be better at adapting your plans to suit your dog's needs.

The Ride Home

When it comes to car rides, all dogs react a little differently. Some want to stick their head out the window and feel the cool breeze, while others want to cower in the back seat and cry. Unless you live within walking distance of the veterinarian, the goal is to help your dog become comfortable riding in vehicles. The chapter on traveling with your Miniature Dachshund will cover car trips in full detail.

There's no better time to start associating car rides with good things than the very first car trip you take with your pup. It's completely normal for your puppy to be curious or unsure about riding in a car because it's something very new. If possible, enlist the help of a friend or a family member for this first ride. They can help you keep your puppy calm while you drive.

A crate or some type of seatbelt system is best, but a puppy that isn't used to that might not like it right away. Typically, having someone hold a dog for the car ride isn't particularly safe, but it's acceptable until your dog is more comfortable with its surroundings. The driver should never be responsible for watching the dog—a distracted driver doesn't make for a safe trip home.

If your little passenger is nervous, speak in a calm, reassuring voice. Avoid talking in a high pitched squeal—this sends signals to the dog that there's something it should be excited about. Soft petting and encouraging words should help your dog feel safe.

At the end of the car ride, reward your dog with a treat. Even if the ride didn't go smoothly, it'll have more time in the future to become accustomed to the car. Make sure to end the first trip on a positive note with plenty of praise and treats.

Photo Courtesy of
Anita Dimon

The First Day

During your first hours with your dog, you want to find the right balance between play time and alone time. You want to spend enough time with your dog to make it feel comfortable in the home, but give it enough space to learn how to cope when it's alone.

Give your dog a moment to walk around the area you've set up for it. Take it on a little tour of its outside bathroom area and reward it for staying calm. Next, slowly integrate toys and other family members into the mix. Don't bombard your puppy with too much excitement at once or it might become overstimulated. Keep things light and fun.

While you'll probably want to have your puppy at your side at all moments during the first couple of days, it's fine to take your eyes off of it for a few minutes here and there, as long as it's in a safe, contained area.

If you plan on being gone during the day on most days, keep in mind that this will be a big change for your dog if you've been holding onto it ever since you brought it home. Puppies have issues with isolation, so leaving them home when you go to work after a full weekend of non-stop play can be tough.

The first night might be a challenge for you and your dog. If you have a new puppy, it might have a hard time settling down for bed. But it's best to set up a bedtime routine that you can stick to. Start by giving your Miniature Dachshund some time outside. A short walk around the block can use up a little excess energy while encouraging it to empty its tiny bladder. Once it's done its business, have it lie down in its bed or in the crate. Eventually, it'll settle down and sleep.

You may find that your new puppy whines a lot while you're in bed. It probably isn't used to sleeping without being surrounded by its mother and siblings. Plus, if the owner is sleeping, the puppy isn't getting any attention. Of course, this noise can be irritating in the wee hours of the morning. To help with this, try keeping your dog close to you—either place its bed right outside of your door or in your bedroom. It may be telling you that it needs to go to the bathroom, and that should not be ignored.

Some owners may find the sounds so detrimental to their sleep that they put their puppy in a far corner of the house so they can't hear it. They may think that they're teaching their dog to "self soothe" but instead they're sending the message that its needs will go unnoticed. Plus, if you can't hear your dog signaling to you that it needs to use the bathroom, you've missed out on a teaching moment.

For the first few weeks, expect to be woken up a few times. If it's been a few hours since your dog has relieved itself, go outside and see if that fixes the problem. Once it is finished, have it go back to bed. If it starts whining immediately after going out, then there's a chance it's just feeling lonely. Try to move it into a position where it can see you and see if this helps calm its nerves.

After enough time, your Miniature Dachshund will grow accustomed to sleeping through the night and its bladder will grow so it won't need to be let out as often. Eventually, you'll be able to move your dog's bed to another spot in the house. Just remember that a dog this tiny needs to use the bathroom a lot, so if it is crying in the middle of the night, it's likely that that is the problem. Try your best to solve the problem first before resorting to earplugs.

The first few days can be stressful and scary, but they can also be fun and exciting. It's fun to watch your Miniature Dachshund grow and develop from a tiny puppy to a full grown dog. It may seem difficult at this stage, but before long you'll have fond memories of the early days.

Photo Courtesy of
Wendy Dryerre

Photo Courtesy of
Rhianne Wilkins

Puppy's First Veterinarian Visit

One of the first things to do between finding your perfect Miniature Dachshund and bringing it home is to find the right veterinarian. Your vet will play a large role in your dog's health. He or she will be a helpful resource and perhaps the first person you go to with questions about your dog. Because you'll want to have a good relationship, it's important to find the right one.

If you live in a city, then you probably have a few options for which clinic to visit. Just like with any business, you'll find that some are better suited for your needs than others. If you have no idea where to start when looking for a vet, here are a few tips.

Perhaps the easiest way to find a vet is to take recommendations from people who know dogs the best. Breeders spend lots of time at the vet, so if you purchase your pup from a local Miniature Dachshund breeder, they might be able to give you a good recommendation. Animal shelters typically have good relationships with a nearby vet, so that's another good option. Finally, talk to other dog owners in your area. They can tell you the good things (and the bad) about the different clinics near you.

Otherwise, a simple web search is a good starting point. Look at the websites and see if these clinics have the things you're looking for. Do they have hours that work with your schedule? Do they specialize in dogs and other small pets? Do the employees have a lot of good experience? Out of all the clinics in the area, choose a few that look like they might fit your needs.

If you're still having a hard time narrowing things down, ask a few contenders if you can visit their facilities and meet the staff. Once there, make sure that everything looks clean and tidy. There should be no overwhelming odors. If timely treatments and lab results are important to you, make sure the clinic has their own lab, x-ray, and surgery rooms. Otherwise, tests and procedures may be referred to other facilities.

Finally, take a moment to chat with the staff. You want to get the impression that they're respected in their field and friendly to talk to. You'll be spending some time with them over the course of your dog's life, so you'll want to make sure you get along well with them.

Once you've made your decision, you might want to bring your pooch in for a friendly visit. Dogs are often scared of the vet because it's a strange place to be. It can be scary for a dog to stand on a metal table while being poked and prodded by a stranger. Forming positive associations with the vet can help the experience not to be so scary. Drive to the office and let your puppy meet the vet without having to be examined. Afterwards, give it a treat for handling the situation.

Even if you don't bring your dog in for a visit, you'll need to schedule an appointment with your veterinarian soon after bringing your dog home, whether it's for your breeder's health guarantee or just for vaccinations. A smooth vet visit is possible with plenty of preparation.

First, make sure your puppy is okay with car travel. Once that is covered, make sure it is comfortable with being touched. Run your hands along its back, feeling the abdomen, neck, legs, and feet. Look inside of the ears and pull the lips back to expose the teeth. You want your dog to be used to being touched on certain parts of its body. After the trip to the vet, reward your dog with lots of play time and treats.

Puppy Training Classes

Within the first few weeks with your new dog, you'll probably want to look into training classes. There's no better time to start training and there are many reasons why a puppy class is a good idea.

First, putting your puppy in a room with other people and dogs is a good way to start the socialization process. It will learn how to behave around others and will become more comfortable and friendly around both people and dogs. The more experience it has, the less likely it is to feel threatened around other dogs.

Also, going to a class every week will give you and your family members a little extra motivation to work hard at training. Not only will you have to devote a set amount of time to work in class, but you'll also want to practice so you can show off your hard work the next week.

Photo Courtesy of Hayley Whytock

Not only can you practice your training skills with others, but you'll be guided by someone with lots of experience. A good trainer can show you how to get started and offer helpful tips if your Mini Dachshund is particularly stubborn.

When looking for a class, the main thing you want to look for is positive training. If a trainer uses methods that include punishment or fear tactics, you should avoid those classes. Dogs learn best through positive reinforcement, so skip out on the trainer that uses controversial methods.

Dog trainers aren't necessarily required to do coursework before they can teach classes, but you still want to make sure the trainer knows what they're doing. When looking for a trainer, ask what classes they've taken, how long they've been working with dogs, and if they have any experience with breeds like the Miniature Dachshund. Different breeds have different learning requirements, so you'll want to ensure that they can handle your Mini Dachshund.

Once you find the best trainer and the right class, you're all set. Who knows, maybe you and your puppy will make new friends in the process!

Getting Supplies Ready

There are a lot of upfront costs associated with a new dog. Some things, like crates and dishes, will probably only need to be purchased once. Other things, like toys and treats, require frequent purchases. To make your life easier, collect the things your new dog needs before it comes home. Here are a few items your new dog will need immediately:

Your dog will need two sturdy bowls, one for water and one for food. While plastic bowls may be inexpensive, they can easily be nibbled to pieces by a Mini Dachshund. Small stainless steel dishes should do the trick. You'll also want to buy small treats for training. Most importantly, you'll want to buy a dog food that your Mini Dachshund will eat. The best bet is to start with whatever food it ate at the breeder's house or at the shelter since your dog will already be used to it. If you decide to switch foods, you can slowly transition later.

Next, your dog will need a place to sleep. While many dog owners just choose to use a dog bed, a crate is a wonderful place for your dog to get some alone time. Whichever you choose, give your dog a soft, comfortable place to rest. You'll be teaching it to go to that same spot every night.

In order to go on daily walks, your pup will need a collar and leash. Because this breed is so small, make sure the collar you purchase is small enough not to be slipped out of. It should be neither uncomfortably tight, nor too loose. A good rule of thumb is to be able to fit two fingers between the collar and the dog's neck. Harnesses are a good option for dogs that tend to wiggle out of collars. You'll also need a four-foot or six-foot leash. When your dog becomes more experienced at walking on a leash, a longer leash may be acceptable, but in the beginning, start with something that can keep it close to you.

You'll also need a few grooming products on hand to ensure your dog looks and feels good. A brush is necessary for removing excess fur and keeping long coats tangle-free. A toothbrush and special toothpaste for dogs keeps your Miniature Dachshund's pearly whites healthy. Nail clippers keep your dog from sinking its long claws into your furniture, while keeping its feet comfortable. Finally, it's always good to have some dog shampoo on hand in case your Miniature Dachshund gets dirty.

Toys are a necessary item for your dog to have. All dogs like to chew, and if you don't give them something acceptable to sink their teeth into, they will choose one of your belongings as a chew toy. Sturdy, well-made stuffed toys will keep your little hunter entertained for hours. Strong rubber toys or nylon chewing bones help your puppy with teething and keep it busy. When choosing a toy, make sure that it doesn't have small pieces that can detach and cause your dog to choke. You'd be surprised how easily a little Mini Dachshund can destroy a toy.

Depending on the layout of your home, you'll probably need just a few more things to dog-proof your house or apartment. If you have a large house that a Miniature Dachshund could become lost in, a wire pen or a few strategically placed baby gates can make all the difference. Especially if you have a puppy, you'll want a few potty pads and enzymatic cleaning products to deal with accidents.

While it may feel like you're going on a massive shopping spree to get ready for your dog, remember that some items will last you a long time. Buy quality items that cannot break and cause your dog injury, or be destroyed by tiny teeth.

Cost Breakdown for the First Year

Now that you have a better idea of what you will need to buy for your dog right away, let's take a look at how much this will all cost. Depending on where you live and what items you buy, this cost can vary. But here's a rough estimate of what you may expect to spend during the first year.

First, let's start with the dog itself. If you get your Miniature Dachshund from a dog shelter or Dachshund rescue, you're looking at a fee of around $200-$300. This typically includes necessary vaccinations, neutering or spay surgery, and micro chipping.

If you're planning on buying from a reputable breeder, expect to pay anywhere from $500 to over $1,000 depending on coat and color type. These pups will usually have their first vaccinations, but they will not be spayed or neutered.

Next, consider professional help, like vet visits and dog trainers. Plan to spend anywhere between $200-$500 a year for basic veterinary care, depending on where you live and what kind of healthcare your dog requires. If you plan on taking puppy training classes, these will run you a couple hundred dollars more.

Most of your expenses for supplies will come when you buy your dog. Leashes, beds, crates, and food dishes can add up. Depending on what you purchase, these supplies can run you several hundred dollars.

Finally, you'll be purchasing a lot of dog food for your hungry puppy. Luckily, this breed is so tiny that you'll be spending way less money on food than owners of large dogs. The average dog eats about $300 worth of food a year, so your Miniature Dachshund should be well below this threshold. Depending on what foods you buy, this cost can vary.

On average, pet owners spend over $10,000 during the life of a pet. While this may seem like a lot of money, the love you receive from your dog makes it more than worth it. You can cut costs by purchasing good, sturdy pet products and by practicing preventative health measures.

There's so much to do the first few days and weeks of your dog's life in your home. It can seem like an overwhelming amount of work, but once you get past the early stage, it will get easier and the costs will be fewer. A well-prepared home will make your new Miniature Dachshund feel more safe and secure, and you'll have a little extra peace of mind.

CHAPTER 5
Being a Puppy Parent

"There is so much you can do with these guys: Earth dog competition, conformation shows, agility, barn hunts, obedience, rally, or even a leisurely stroll down a country road."

Reba Mandrell
www.heartlanddachshunds.com

Your Miniature Dachshund will go through a lot of changes during its first year of life. Not only will its tiny body grow and mature, but its behavior will change. If you're bringing home a new puppy from the breeder, you're in for an exciting time watching your dog grow and develop.

However, this will be the most challenging time as a dog owner. Puppies depend on their owners to teach them how they are supposed to behave in the home. Naturally, their little brains need time to develop and make sense of their world. Be prepared for challenges during this time, but keep in mind that all of your hard work will be worth it.

Being a puppy parent is not too unlike raising a young child. You'll have to figure out what your puppy's cries mean, you'll teach it everything it needs to know, and you'll likely have to clean up a good number of "accidents" around the house. It's exhausting work, but at the end of the day you'll get to cuddle with a Mini Dachshund that loves you.

Standing by Your Expectations

Dogs don't have the same ability to reason that humans do, so the things you teach about living in the home need to be taught in language a dog can understand.

For example, if you don't mind when your dog sits on the old grey sofa with you but you don't want it sitting on the nice, white sofa, it's going to be hard to teach a puppy that one sofa is acceptable and the other is not. To a dog, both sofas look like perfectly comfortable places to sit, and it couldn't care less about how clean or expensive they were.

In this situation, you must decide which is more important: having your dog sit on one couch with you, or keeping your other one off limits.

Your dog will become confused if it can sometimes sit on the couch, but sometimes cannot sit on the couch.

For this reason, it's important to decide with the members of your household which rules you'd like to enforce, and which rules are less important to you.

Once you decide on a rule, everyone must stick to it. If you correct your dog when it tries to jump on you but your partner encourages that behavior, it's going to be much more difficult to correct it in the future. Everyone needs to know the rules and abide by them every time.

Also, keep in mind that you cannot correct your dog after the fact. If your dog chews up your pillow, it is not capable of making a connection between your destroyed belongings and its actions hours after it happened. You can only put a stop to misbehavior if you catch your dog in the act of misbehaving.

For this reason, it's important to have someone watching your puppy as much as possible. There are so many learning moments during the day, but if you put your dog outside for hours on end and forget about it, then your dog doesn't have the chance to learn what you expect from it.

With lots of repetition, your puppy will eventually catch on to your rules. From this point, it's just a matter of reinforcing the rules during your every day life. This stage is difficult, so keep calm and continue practicing.

How to Crate Train

Photo Courtesy of Vanessa Higgins

If you're bringing home a new puppy, you might decide that you want to crate train. Some owners decide not to, and that's perfectly acceptable. However, there are lots of benefits to crate training your puppy.

First, crate training can help with housetraining. Typically, dogs do not want to soil their living space. When your dog is in a crate at night, it is more likely to hold it until you let it out to use the bathroom in the morning.

Second, a crate is a good method of transportation for your dog. Whether you're taking it to the vet or on a weekend trip, your dog is much safer riding

47

in a well-restrained crate than running loose in the car. Also, if your dog tends to suffer from car sickness, placing the crate on the floor away from windows may ease its suffering.

Finally, a crate is a safe place for your dog to go if it gets stressed out. Your Mini Dachshund may be a friendly pup around large groups of people, but sometimes a lot of action can be overstimulating. If your dog feels like its crate is a safe place to go, it is likely to chill out for a while. Stress is not good for dogs; a dog with a safe place to go when it feels stressed is less likely to act out in different ways.

Crates should not be used as punishment or doggie jail. When your dog associates the crate with negative feelings, it will be difficult to get it to sleep or travel in it. A crate should always be a nice, happy place to hang out.

Some dogs are just naturally a little wary of climbing into a strange container. That's why you need to let them explore it on their own time at first. Put a comfortable blanket or dog bed inside and drop a few treats in there. If your pup still doesn't take the bait, try making a trail of treats leading up to the crate.

If you find that your Miniature Dachshund is still not interested, give it time. A curious puppy will eventually try to explore the crate. The thing you don't want to do is force it into the crate. If it decides it doesn't like this sudden bombardment, it may never approach the crate again.

Once your dog explores the crate, try keeping it in there for longer periods of time. Place toys or even food dishes inside so it will have a reason to spend some time in there. Once you feel like it is comfortable inside the crate, try shutting the gate for short periods of time. Eventually, you'll be able to extend crate time until it no longer wants to get out. Of course, only close the door to the crate when it's absolutely necessary. Your dog should not be spending hours on end in a closed crate.

Chewing

All dogs, but puppies especially, like to chew. For puppies, chewing is how they sense the world and work out baby teeth. If you do not teach dogs which objects are okay to chew on and which ones aren't, they'll sink their teeth into anything they can find.

If you find that your Miniature Dachshund has a chewing problem, there are a few possible reasons. Once you find the problem, it's easier to work out a solution for your dog. If your puppy has yet to lose its baby teeth, it might have a lot of pain or discomfort. Like a teething baby, a puppy needs durable toys to chew so its adult teeth can poke through.

Maybe your puppy is just curious and wants to explore your belongings. If this is what's happening, it may not be destructive chewing, but just "mouthing". Your dog may even try to do this with your hands. While playful biting is usually not a malicious behavior, you want to teach your dog that biting can hurt. If it sinks its teeth into your hand, say "ouch" like a yelping dog would. It'll probably react like it would if its litter mates were correcting its behavior.

Finally, your dog might destroy your things because it is bored, has too much energy, or has separation anxiety. Try giving your dog a little more exercise during the day. A tired dog is much less destructive than a rambunctious puppy.

If your smart little Mini Dachshund gets bored easily, try to find toys that have a puzzle aspect to them. There are some chew toys on the market that allow you to hide treats in them. Then, your dog must solve the puzzle to get the treats out. Not only does it keep your dog busy, but also it allows it to use its teeth. These kinds of toys are great if you work during the day and your Miniature Dachshund is home alone.

If you're still having troubles with chewing, there are other methods you may try. If your dog likes to chew on furniture, there are taste deterrents sold in pet stores that can help. These are sprays that are not harmful for your dog, but do not taste good. After enough attempts, your dog may decide that it really doesn't want to chew on the legs of your table after all.

If you catch your dog in the act of chewing, you'll want to correct it and offer an alternative. For example, if your dog has a hold of your shoe, get its attention with a clap or the "drop it" command. Distract it long enough for it to lose interest in what it already has, in order to switch out your shoe for its bone. Any time it chooses one of its toys over one of your belongings to chew, give lots of praise.

Your Noisy Puppy

When it comes to vocalizations, you can't expect your dog to always be perfectly silent. Dogs will bark from time to time. However, it is understandably annoying if your dog barks constantly. So you'll want to teach your dog how to control its voice.

Dogs bark for a variety of reasons. Some bark because they're trying to warn their owners about other people and animals. Some dogs bark for attention. Other times, dogs might bark because they're excited and don't know what else to do with their energy.

If you have a little watchdog, you may try to eliminate whatever is causing the barking. If your dog likes to watch from the window, you may want to place it in a different room when the barking starts. Then it will realize that the barking causes it to lose window privileges.

You may also try to command it to do something that is incompatible with barking. If your dog likes to bark when someone rings the doorbell, you can command it to lie down on its bed. If it's away from the action in a prone position, it's harder to bark.

Finally, you want to make sure that you don't accidentally encourage the barking. If your dog barks for attention and you yell or plead with it to stop, this is seen as attention. In this case, try to ignore the barking completely. Your dog will discover that it gets no reward or feedback from you for this behavior, removing its motivation.

Whining is another common puppy behavior that can grate on an owner's nerves. Whining may be a sign that there is something wrong with your pup. When you bring your dog home, note what is happening when your dog is whining. It may be trying to tell you that it needs to go to the bathroom. It also may be communicating that something is upsetting it. Sometimes, it just wants a little attention.

If you find that your dog is whining purely to get attention, use the same methods suggested for barking for attention. Do your best to completely ignore it. Stay quiet, and even turn your back to your dog. When it stops, you can give it praise or attention. Just make sure that something isn't wrong before ignoring its cries.

Growling is another noise that dogs make, but this one should never be ignored. Growling is how dogs tell others to get away before they snap. If you hear your dog growling, stop whatever you're doing and back away. Once you know what causes your dog to growl, you can work towards eliminating stressors and making your dog feel safe and comfortable.

Digging

Dachshunds were born to dig. They were specifically bred to be great at burrowing to catch animals in the ground. However, if your dog lives in the house, digging probably won't be appreciated.

There are two common methods to stop inappropriate digging. First, you can ban all types of digging in and around your home. With this method, you'll have to catch your dog in the act and correct the unwanted behavior. If you distract it from digging and it stops, reward it.

The other method is to allow digging in certain areas only. This can be tricky to teach if your dog can't tell the difference between your flower garden and its special sandbox. With this method, you need a special dirt pile or sandbox for digging. Reward your dog when it digs in the appropriate spot and correct it when it digs in the wrong spot.

Another way to control digging is by teaching a command to dig. This way, it can also learn "no dig." This gives the owner a little more control.

Separation Anxiety

Photo Courtesy of
Rhianne Wilkins

Separation anxiety happens to a lot of dogs that are adjusting to a new home and new owner. When left untreated, it can lead to increased levels of stress hormones in the body. Anxiety is bad for both the physical and mental health of your dog and can have long-lasting consequences.

If you notice that your dog displays unwanted behaviors despite success in training, these may be symptoms of separation anxiety. An anxious dog may have more accidents in the house, be destructive, attempt to escape, cry and bark excessively, or pant heavily for no reason.

Your Miniature Dachshund was accustomed to a certain way of life before entering your care. A sudden change can be confusing and scary for a dog.

If you bring your dog home and play with it all weekend, the first day you go back to work may be a struggle. Your puppy may feel like you've abandoned it because you're suddenly not around. To help prevent this fear, take small breaks away from your dog at first. Leave it in its pen while doing the laundry or making dinner out of sight. Then, extend the amount of time spent away and leave the house briefly to do your grocery shopping or go to the gym. That way, when you need to be gone for four hours at a time, your dog won't feel as much shock.

Also, do your best to keep your dog calm when you leave and when you enter the house after an absence. If you give your Dachshund hugs and kisses when you leave and make a big scene, then your absence will be a bigger deal. Similarly, if you demand that your dog get excited when you return, it will also be more anxious for your return. Stay calm when you enter and exit the house, and your dog will think nothing of it.

If you've tried to alleviate your dog's anxiety and it's starting to take a toll on its health, you may want to speak with a veterinarian. The vet can offer suggestions or even prescribe medication if nothing else works.

Running Away

If your dog isn't used to your home, it may want to escape and explore the world around it. If your dog had a previous home, it may try to get out to return to the familiar place. If you cannot catch your dog before it escapes, this can result in danger for your dog.

If your dog is in the backyard unsupervised, make sure there is no way it can escape through gaps in the fence. Because Miniature Dachshunds are skilled diggers, you'll want to regularly check to make sure that it hasn't burrowed an escape route.

If your dog is a bundle of energy, it may be more likely to bolt at the first sign of an open door. Regular walks and playtime can help reduce the urge to get out and run.

If your dog gets out, fight the instinct to chase it. It will think this is a fun game and repeat the behavior as often as possible. Try to stay calm and call your dog back to you.

Bedtime

In order for your dog to settle into your household, routines are necessary. One routine that can create stability is a regular bedtime.

When you have a new puppy, it might not accept the fact that you need sleep, too. If you are crate training your dog, then this is a good time to get it to settle into the crate for bed. If not, teach it the "lie down" command for when it's time to go to bed.

Early on, your puppy may whine after you turn the lights off. Because it can't see you or hear you, it may feel abandoned. The resulting whining can be irritating when people are trying to sleep.

First, make sure that your dog is not whining because it needs to use the bathroom. Puppies, especially the smaller breeds, have tiny bladders and need to go out often.

If this is not the issue, try moving the crate or dog bed to your room. That way, your puppy can see you. However, if this disrupts your sleep, you might move it to a nearby room. That way, you'll hear its cries to go out, but it won't be licking your face in the middle of the night.

As long as you know its other needs are met, you may have to tough out the crying for a few weeks. Eventually, your puppy will become more comfortable in your home and it will stop.

Leaving Your Dog Home Alone

If you have to leave the home for work, your dog will have to spend some time alone. For older dogs, this isn't a big issue, as their bladders allow them to hold their urine for several hours. Puppies have more needs that need to be addressed during the day.

Young dogs have a lot of energy and don't know the appropriate outlets for this energy. A bored, energetic dog will become destructive if left alone for too long. To combat this, make sure your dog gets a walk or some quality playtime when you're home.

If your dog is having accidents after a few hours, you may decide to use some sort of alternative indoor bathroom. These work well for small pets because they tend to spend more time inside.

If your puppy is having a hard time with your absence, consider hiring a dog walker or pet sitter to visit once a day. Depending on your pet's needs, you can hire someone to take your Mini Dachshund on a long walk or just to let it use the bathroom and play a little. Having a friendly face show up once a day may keep your puppy entertained enough to feel secure in your home.

This is the most difficult time to care for a dog, but the most exciting. It's completely normal to feel exhausted or frustrated by your new dog. Don't give up! With lots of repetition and practice, your Miniature Dachshund will become acclimated to your home.

CHAPTER 6
Housetraining

"Be Consistent. They will make mistakes but keep going and keep them on a schedule. Having set feeding times will help you keep track of when they will need to go potty. Every 10-15 minutes after eating and drinking and as soon as they wake up."

Roberta LaCosse
www.havendachs.weebly.com

Perhaps the first thing you need to teach a new puppy is how to successfully go to the bathroom outside. Housetraining is no easy task—Mini Dachshunds are intelligent, but they can be rather stubborn. They need lots of practice before they can make it through the day without any accidents.

All puppies have tiny bladders, but Mini Dachshunds have especially tiny bladders. This means that they need to go outside frequently. With time, they'll grow and develop and toilet training will get easier.

Different Options for Potty Training

The most obvious place for a dog to use the bathroom is outside in a grassy area. This requires the least amount of cleanup for owners and is easy for dogs to learn. Because there is such a noticeable difference between the home and outside, your dog will pick up cues that it is allowed to use the bathroom any time it is outside. A backyard is an ideal place for your dog to go because it doesn't require a human to be present. If you don't have a yard, your dog will have to learn to do its business during walks.

However, some owners choose to use different potty training methods that allow their dog to use the bathroom inside the house in a sanitary manner. Many new puppy owners will place newspaper in their puppy's pen to protect the floor from messes. Dogs generally dislike soiling their living quarters, so newspapers in a corner of their pen may be a good place for them to tinkle. Once soiled, the newspapers can be thrown away and replaced easily.

Potty pads are frequently used for puppies. These are large, absorbent pads that can be attached to the floor. Often times, they have special scents that make them attractive toilets for dogs. These keep your floor clean, but must be disposed of each time they get soiled. They are a little more absorbent than newspaper, but they cost more.

There are also other products that don't rely on disposable pads. These indoor potties resemble litter boxes or turf that mimics real grass and are designed to be easy to clean and sanitize. These are more permanent options for owners who will continue to let their dogs use the bathroom indoors after they've been successfully potty trained. These work well with small dogs like Miniature Dachshunds because they can easily be tucked into an obscure corner of the house. They're also a good alternative for owners who live in apartments or owners who cannot always leave the home.

The process for teaching your dog to use these products is the same as for outdoor potty training. If you choose to create an indoor toilet for your dog, think about the right place to put it. A bathroom or laundry room is a good place because it is out of sight and won't stink up the rest of your home. While your dog might spend a lot of time in the kitchen or living room, you probably don't want its excrement in those places.

The First Few Weeks

The first few weeks are always the hardest. You should expect and prepare for accidents as long as the first couple months with your puppy. Keep plenty of towels and cleaning solution on hand, and a positive attitude.

Photo Courtesy of
Ian Fletcher

Photo Courtesy of
Jim Braner

A good guideline for how often your Mini Dachshund needs to go outside is one hour for every month of age. For example, a four month old dog can hold it for about four hours before it needs to use the bathroom. But just to be safe, you can take your puppy out more frequently.

It's good to settle into a routine early so your dog knows what to expect. When you wake up in the morning, let your dog outside before you do anything else, then take it out every hour or so, depending on how old it is. Finally, let it out once more before you put it to bed. As your dog grows, you can reduce the frequency of bathroom breaks.

With regular feeding times come regular bathroom times. Aim to feed your Miniature Dachshund at the same time each day to make its bathroom breaks more predictable. If you leave for work in the morning, make sure you give your dog plenty of time to eat and potty before you go.

Do your best to observe your puppy's habits and warning signs. Some dogs will be playing one minute and peeing on the floor the next without any warning. Others will whine, giving you a short window to take them out. Some may even scratch at the ground or circle. If you can spot the signs that your dog needs to go, it will make training much easier.

When you take your dog outside, try to take it to the same spot every time. This will help trigger its brain to realize it is supposed to be using the bathroom. It's also nice to have it use the same spot because it makes cleanup easier for you, plus your dog will naturally use a spot where it recognizes its own scent.

When starting out, instead of releasing your puppy into the yard, you may want to put it on the leash. That way, you have control of where it goes. You can take it directly to its bathroom spot without worrying about it getting too distracted by everything that's going on outside.

Rewarding Positive Behavior

When it comes to any kind of training, positivity is key. Any time your dog uses the bathroom is a training moment. Luckily for a new puppy owner, there is no shortage of training moments!

Use whatever rewards motivate your pup. Treats are an obvious choice but praise and playtime work too. If your dog makes it to the potty spot and successfully uses it, this deserves a reward. Make your puppy feel good for doing exactly what you want it to do. Over time, your dog will make the connection between the behavior and the reward.

If your dog doesn't make it to the bathroom, there's not much you can do besides clean it up and try again next time. If you see your dog about to have an accident, you can try to quickly transport it to the bathroom spot.

Sometimes, you may take your dog outside at a regular potty break interval and it will refuse to go. Try to give it a little time to sniff out its surroundings. However, it should use the bathroom before it is allowed to play. Once it goes, a game of fetch or a walk can be a nice reward that also provides good exercise.

Training should always be positive. Punishment can result in unwanted behaviors and can upset your dog. Despite your frustrations, do your best to keep a happy disposition with your dog. Dogs can sense their owners' emotions.

In the Event of an Accident

Let's face it—your new puppy is bound to have an accident at some point. In fact, a really little puppy may have a lot of accidents. Don't worry! As their brains and bodies mature, dogs become better at housetraining.

If you can catch your dog in the act of having an accident, you can try to get its attention to let it know that it's doing something you don't want it to do. A clap or a firm "hey" may get its attention. If it stops, you can quickly get it to its bathroom and let it finish. Sometimes, it's too late. Try not to get upset, as your dog may become upset too.

It's a common fallacy that if you find one of your dog's messes, you should rub its nose in it. Not only is this upsetting to your dog, but there is no logic behind it. Dogs do not have a memory like humans do. They are incapable of connecting a past action (pooping on the rug) with the present moment (my owner is yelling at me).

In fact, punishing your dog by yelling and physical punishments will cause your dog to hide its accidents from you. Instead of letting you know when it needs to go, it will fear you and choose to hide in a corner of your home to relieve itself. Once you've lost your dog's trust, it can be hard to regain.

If your dog has an accident while you are gone, clean the spot well. If a dog can smell the site of a past accident, then it may be keen to go there again. You can purchase enzymatic cleaning products that will remove the scent.

If your dog is exiting its puppy stage and is still having accidents, there may be other factors at work. Separation anxiety can cause accidents in otherwise well-trained dogs. Males that have yet to be neutered may lift their leg in order to mark their territory. If your dog tinkles on the carpet when guests come over, maybe it's just too excited. If you can't pinpoint the problem, talk to a veterinarian. They can help you figure out if your dog's accidents are behavioral or medical in nature.

Crate Training, Pens, and Doggy Doors

Photo Courtesy of Vince DiGuglielmo

Crate training is helpful for housetraining because a crate is a contained area for your dog to spend time in. If your dog is in a small space, it is less likely to soil its living quarters than if it has the full run of the house.

Also, night is prime time for accidents because it's the longest your dog will go without being let out. If it's in a crate it may still have an accident, but at least you'll be able to find the mess quickly. If you keep the crate near you while you sleep, you'll be able to hear your dog's cries to be let out to go to the bathroom.

The key is finding the right size of crate. Your Miniature Dachshund will need a tiny crate. The crate should be large enough that your dog can stand up and turn around. However, if there is a lot of extra space, it may be comfortable using the bathroom in the crate.

If you choose not to crate train your dog, you will still want some method of keeping your dog contained. For a small breed like Miniature Dachshunds, wire pens work well. These give them plenty of space to stretch their legs and play. At the same time, it keeps them from running and hiding around your house. You'll be able to protect your floor with newspapers or potty pads so you won't have to newspaper your entire home.

If you want to give your dog even more room to roam, you can install gates around your house. This way, you can limit your dog to one or two rooms. This is helpful if you'd like to allow your dog to be comfortable with all parts of the house, but you have a few spaces you want to keep off-limits.

Finally, if you have a fenced-in backyard, there's also the possibility of installing a doggy door in your home. This is helpful if you may not always be available to let your dog out when it needs to go.

However, there are a couple drawbacks to having a doggy door. If your dog can go in and out as it pleases, that means that it can also take your belongings out and other creatures can come inside. Also, it can be hard to keep tabs on your dog if it can be inside or outside at any time.

If you go with this method, you'll need to teach your dog how to go in and out. Some dogs are hesitant to crawl in and out without a little incentive. If you can get your dog to exit, give it a treat. If it uses the bathroom after exiting the door, give it another treat.

Housetraining Adult Dogs

If you've adopted your adult Miniature Dachshund, there's always a possibility that it wasn't properly housetrained. Depending on its former home life, it may also have anxieties that make it more prone to having accidents. Fortunately, most adopted dogs will have some housetraining experience. But your newly adopted pup may need a little refresher course.

The same rules for housetraining puppies apply to adult dogs, too. With adults, it may be easier because they have larger bladders. You may want to take them out more often to start, but once they get the hang of your household, four to five toilet trips a day will suffice.

If you have a particularly stubborn Miniature Dachshund, it will need extra positive reinforcement. Make sure it gets extra treats for using the bathroom in the predetermined spot and lots of playtime once it's finished. It might have an accident or two at first, but once it is comfortable in its new home, it'll have no problem adjusting to its new bathroom.

Once you and your pup have mastered housetraining, puppy care gets much easier. If you find that your Miniature Dachshund is stubborn, don't get frustrated. If your dog senses your frustration, it might try to fight you on being trained. Give plenty of treats and love when it does a good job and keep your cool when it has accidents.

CHAPTER 7
Socialization

"As a rule, Miniature Dachshunds get along well with other animals. However, it will depend on how much socialization the dog gets at a young age. A new puppy should be socialized with other dogs, cats, children, household noises, etc..."

Lori Noland
www.drycreekminidachshunds.com

Once your Miniature Dachshund is comfortable in its new home, it's time to get it accustomed to the world outside the house. Socialization is the process of getting your dog to feel comfortable around people and other dogs. This part of raising a dog can be overlooked, but it's just as important as obedience training.

This chapter will cover the basics of good socialization skills in dogs and tips for helping your dog feel more comfortable around others. If your dog feels safe, it's more likely to behave how you want it to. Good socialization can make life easier for both the Miniature Dachshund and the owner.

Photo Courtesy of Sue Forrest

The Benefits of Socialization

As humans, we know it's not healthy to have excessive stress. Whether our stress comes from our household responsibilities or our jobs, we know that stress can affect our mental and physical health in negative ways. Still, many owners don't consider that their dogs can experience the same type of stress from their surroundings.

When dogs feel stressed, a surge of stress hormones flows through their bloodstream. These chemicals trigger the "fight or flight" response. They feel as though they must defend themselves against the stressor or avoid it. As humans, we know that their fears aren't always rational. But to your dog, the stranger at the door could be a dangerous person. When the danger is real these chemicals can save your dog's life. When the danger isn't real they can wreak havoc on its body.

When stress hormones are frequently created by the body, this can begin to affect the organs. Regular stress can put a strain on your dog's immune system. When the immune system is under pressure, it makes it harder for the body to fight off disease and infection.

Stress can lead to mental health issues, too. If your dog experiences the same stressors frequently, it may develop a problem with anxiety. Little things can upset dogs with anxiety, causing them to act out.

Not only is your dog's stress dangerous for the dog itself, it can be dangerous for others as well. If your dog chooses the fight response, someone can get hurt. It seems counterintuitive, but dogs are most dangerous when they are scared. When seriously frightened, they will use their teeth to protect themselves. The dog may think that a bite will keep a stranger from hurting it, but sometimes the stranger just wants to pet it.

If your dog is well socialized, stress is less of a concern. Because it is used to being around others, it won't have the same fears as an unsocialized dog would. As an owner, this makes life a little easier when you don't have to constantly worry about the welfare of your dog. Instead, you can both enjoy meeting all the great people and pooches this world has to offer.

Socialization with Other Dogs

Despite being part of the same species, it's not uncommon for dogs to feel nervous around other dogs. If your dog spends most of its time in the home, it might not get the opportunity to spend time with other dogs.

As a breed, Miniature Dachshunds are moderately friendly with other dogs. But remember that these little guys are fearless. They may get themselves into trouble with other dogs and be too courageous to back down from a challenge. With regular socialization, though, they can learn to behave themselves around the big dogs.

Dogs interact in different ways. If you watch dogs interact, you'll find that there is a lot of sniffing going on. Dogs can pick up more information through scent than what even seems possible. With just a few sniffs of another dog's bottom, they can tell the sex of the other dog to find out if it's a friend or a mating competitor.

You might also see a dog playfully bite another dog. This isn't necessarily done to cause pain and it isn't always rough play. Dogs use their mouths to touch, so gentle biting is a way for dogs to communicate. Dogs can use their body language to initiate play, assert dominance, or let other dogs know when they're playing too roughly. Humans may not recognize what is happening, but dogs exchange a lot of information through nonverbal cues.

As an owner, you can let your dog interact with others without intervening. In fact, nervous owners send signals to their dogs that there is danger present. However, it's good to know the signs of trouble so you can help remove your dog from the situation if necessary.

If your dog is experiencing serious fear, it needs to be removed from the situation before it lashes out. The signs of anxiety include excessive panting, crying, staying low to the ground, or tucking the tail between the legs. Yawning, ears that lay flat against the head, a tense body, and bared teeth are also signs that a dog is upset.

When it's time to socialize your dog, start slowly. If you know someone with a friendly, well-behaved dog, you may invite them to a play date on neutral ground. Give the dogs an opportunity to check each other out and observe your dog's reaction. If it's too much, try again another time. If it does well with several different meetings, it may feel comfortable in a setting with more dogs.

A group obedience course or a dog park are other good places to socialize your dog. You'll be able to supervise your dog while letting it explore many different types of dogs. Just remember to start slowly and never rush your dog into socializing with others, especially when it's showing signs of anxiety.

Socializing with Other Pets

Socialization is especially important for your new Miniature Dachshund if there are already other pets living in your home. If your dog cannot become socialized, then there will be lasting issues in your household. However, Miniature Dachshunds are generally good with other pets, as long as they have a chance to make themselves comfortable in your home.

Just like with any type of socialization, it's best not to rush into things. Whether your home includes dogs, cats, or both, you'll want to give your pets plenty of time to become acquainted.

Dogs can become territorial and possessive of their belongings, so plan your first meeting in a neutral place. If possible, find someone to help you with your other dogs. It can be tricky to make the introductions by yourself.

Photo Courtesy of Mel Neild

Once you feel comfortable with how your current dogs are behaving with your new dog, repeat the process at home. Keep everyone on a leash until they can be trusted. This is also a good time to utilize your wire pens and baby gates.

Socializing with cats is a little trickier. The naturally daring Miniature Dachshund probably won't back down from a standoff with a cat, so it's necessary to ensure that your cat is able to escape. If your cat is larger than the Mini Dachshund, that may make getaways a little easier.

The next chapter will include an in-depth look at the process of integrating your new dog into your pet family.

Socializing with Humans

Miniature Dachshunds are fiercely loyal to their human families, but are generally wary of humans they don't know. They aren't the type to cower in fear when a stranger approaches them, but will rather bark and make their presence known. For this reason, it will take some time to make your new dog feel comfortable around you and your family members. Eventually, your Miniature Dachshund will be affectionate with you, but don't expect it to be at first.

By the time you bring your Mini Dachshund home, you should already have a good relationship. Whether it's coming from a breeder or a shelter, you've probably met a few times and maybe even had it visit your home, helping it be able to trust you to ensure that its other introductions are safe.

One great way to get your dog to socialize with others is by inviting friends and family over to meet your new dog. Keep in mind that a whole houseful of people can upset your dog, so keep visitors to one or two guests at a time. This lets your dog meet the people important to you while you get to show off your cute new pup.

When introducing people to your dog (and vice versa) don't force your dog into anyone's arms. Let the dog wander around and sniff people out first. Instruct your houseguests to stay calm and try not to get your dog too riled up at first. If your dog approaches people and behaves appropriately, give it a reward. Your dog should be friendly, but not overly rough or aggressive with anyone. If your dog feels comfortable around the people, give your dog the opportunity to play with them.

Photo Courtesy of Vince DiGuglielmo

If you find that your new dog is seriously distressed by this encounter, let it have a little time out in the crate or another room. Give it a chance to calm down and then try again. You don't want to force your dog into anything that is potentially traumatic. This breed isn't normally skittish, so shyness shouldn't be a big issue.

Having guests over is also a good way to practice proper behavior when the doorbell rings. There's a good chance your Mini Dachshund will show off its booming bark when visitors arrive. Depending on your training methods, you may command your dog to sit in a certain place when the doorbell rings. Or, you can practice the "quiet" command.

When introducing your new dog to other people, one of the main things to remember is to keep things calm and casual. If you don't make a big deal out of having people over, your dog won't either. Dogs often follow our cues for how to react to situations, so if you're calm it will help your dog stay calm, too.

Introducing Your Dog to Your Children

Miniature Dachshunds make good family pets because they tend to get along well with children. Their loyalty to the family will make them feel like it is their duty to protect the kids. Don't tell these dogs that they're too little to protect kids from any real danger—they're fierce and confident dogs.

Introducing your dog to kids is a little different than introducing them to adults. Kids naturally have more energy and don't always know the proper way to act around dogs, so it's the owner's responsibility to educate the children and the dog on appropriate behavior.

Before introducing the dog, talk to the kids about how to treat a dog. Teach them to be gentle, because Miniature Dachshunds are small dogs that can be injured if they are treated roughly. Tell them to be quiet when the puppy is in the room, so it does not become scared. Have them offer your dog a treat if it approaches them without barking or getting too wound up.

Young children always need to be supervised when dogs are present. Even if your Miniature Dachshund turns out to be the sweetest companion, there's no telling what can happen if something goes wrong. Small children can sometimes be rough with dogs, even when they don't mean to hurt them. If a dog gets hurt or scared, its first line of defense is to snap at someone in an effort to warn them. While this warning snap might not always cause physical injury, it's not worth inflicting a fear of dogs on the child. Kids and Miniature Dachshunds go great together, but both can be unpredictable. Your children and dog will both benefit from a little parental supervision.

Good socialization can really improve a dog's quality of life. It also makes an owner's job easier when your Miniature Dachshund can be trusted to behave around other people. When socialization takes place early in a puppy's life, it will have an easier time adapting to all other aspects of adulthood.

CHAPTER 8
Miniature Dachshunds and Other Pets

If your household already contains pets, you need to evaluate how your existing pets will do with a new little family member. If your pets aren't very well socialized with dogs, it's a good idea to work with them before bringing home a new dog. If your old dog has a history of having problems with other dogs, a feisty Miniature Dachshund is not going to help things.

The same goes for cats. A temperamental cat with no dog experience may become stressed if a tiny bundle of energy comes bursting into your house. For the safety of every pet in your household, make sure your existing pets can handle a new friend.

Once your pets are ready, it's time to begin the integration process. This is similar to socialization, but with more at stake. If your Miniature Dachshund gets into a scuffle with a dog at the dog park, you can always remove it from the situation. When your new dog has issues with your other dog, there's a chance that the problem will take longer to resolve.

This process is much easier with puppies. They haven't had a lot of experience in the world yet, so anything you teach them within a positive frame will become second nature to them. With adopted dogs, it can be hard to know if they've been properly socialized and are okay with other pets. But with some work, most dogs can learn to get along with others.

Introducing Your New Puppy

Just like with socialization, you want to start things slowly. As discussed in the last chapter, first meetings should be done on neutral territory. The reason why it's not ideal to take your puppy to your house is because your other dogs have made connections with your home. It's covered with their scent and filled with their toys. A territorial dog may feel threatened if a young pup waltzes onto its turf. A park or open field with plenty of space is a good meeting place.

With the help of another person, put each dog on its own leash and stand with a few feet of space in between you. Give your dogs a minute to see and smell each other. If they behave well, let them approach each other. They will sniff each other for a while as they collect information about each other. With any luck, they may even initiate play or show disinterest.

If they show any signs of anxiety or aggression, calmly make space between them. You don't want to draw too much attention to their reaction, but you certainly don't want a fight to break out. Give them time and space before trying again.

Once your dogs are comfortable with each other at the park, it is time to introduce them in the home. Again, it's helpful to have another person present. Keep both dogs on a leash, just to add a little control. Slowly let them sniff each other again, while watching for signs of fear. Once they have shown you that they can get along while on the leash the extra restraint can be removed.

Just because the first meeting went well doesn't mean the dogs are off the hook. Plan for a probationary period where you keep a close eye on them. Just because they passed the first test doesn't mean that they're automatically best friends. Once they have a chance to play a little, things could change.

During this time, make sure both dogs have the opportunity to go to a safe place if they suddenly feel nervous. Crates are good for this because they can provide an extra layer of protection from the other dog if necessary. You may also want to enforce periods of separation using baby gates. The dogs will still be able to see and smell each other, but they won't be able to get into a conflict while you aren't available to break it up.

If your dogs have made it a few weeks without any incidents, then you can remove the barriers and let them spend more time together.

Photo Courtesy of Vanessa Higgins

The owner plays a large role in making sure dogs continue to get along. Even if your new dog demands a lot of attention, make sure your older dog isn't feeling neglected. A bored dog may act out and cause trouble for your new puppy. Both dogs should have their own beds and toys to prevent fights.

If you're bringing your new Miniature Dachshund into your home with cats, make sure your household has plenty of space for both. While Dachshunds are fairly friendly, they are natural hunters. They love to chase anything that moves. Unfortunately, this includes cats.

But if you feel confident that your cats can handle the change, a young Miniature Dachshund can learn how to be kind to your cats. You may have to work around the natural prey drive, but it's possible for dogs and cats to get along.

When introducing your dog to your cat, the end goal is different. With dogs, you would like them to be able to spend time together and play. With dogs and cats, you just want them to respect the other's space.

Photo Courtesy of
Laura Scott

Because the Miniature Dachshund is so short, a perching spot out of reach for your dog may help create the necessary space. Otherwise, utilize pens, gates, and separate rooms as much as you can. If your dog and cat get into an altercation, your cat needs a place to bolt to where it can feel safe from a rambunctious puppy.

With cats, it's not as important to make introductions on neutral territory. When you bring your dog into the house, keep it on a leash. That way, it will be unable to chase if the instinct kicks in. You don't necessarily need them to be in close contact to check each other out. Just being on opposite sides of a room can be enough for them to get a good sense of each other.

If either animal gets stressed out or too excited, separate them and try again later. Eventually, you want to get to the point where each animal feels indifferent towards the other. If your dog cannot learn to ignore the cat's presence, then it will find tasks that require focus difficult.

Pack Mentality

The effect of social order with dogs is somewhat controversial among dog experts. Some trainers use it as the basis of their theories, while others believe that it has little effect on their dogs. However, it's something to be aware of when taking care of multiple dogs and may help explain why they act the way they do.

In the wild, dogs are social animals that live in packs. Within these packs are different roles. Just like in a group of humans, there are leaders and followers. Different personalities play different roles in a social setting.

In a dog pack, personalities are usually described as dominant or submissive. The degrees of dominance and submission vary within the social order. A dominant dog is a leader. A submissive dog is a follower. In the wild, these roles are put into place so the pack can survive harsh conditions.

There's a good chance your domesticated dog will never have to face the same challenges a wild dog must. It probably doesn't need to hunt to eat or find shelter. It's possible that some of the pack instinct is hidden somewhere within your dog, but with the domesticated dog, things are a little different. In fact, you may even be able to claim the "alpha" position in your home!

Just because dogs are dominant and submissive in a pack doesn't mean that these roles can never change. Even in the wild, dominance and submission are on a sliding scale. For instance, a dog can be dominant in one relationship and submissive in another.

These are not hard and fast rules that will determine your dog's personality around others. Dominant doesn't mean aggressive and mean, just like submissive doesn't necessarily mean scared and anxious. When it comes to your pack, don't be surprised if your Miniature Dachshund tries to take over the role of top dog—Dachshunds are confident, stubborn dogs.

However, your Miniature Dachshund should never outrank a human. It needs to be able to take commands from people. It may be the ringleader within your dog family, but not when the owner is present.

If you notice your dog is dominant or submissive within a group of dogs, this doesn't have too much bearing on any other factor in its life. It can still have a good life regardless of where it ranks on any given day.

Small Breed Psychology

If you've spent enough time around different dog breeds, you may have observed that there are often behavioral differences in dogs according to size. This observation is so common that it's often referred to as "small dog syndrome".

This refers to the belief that small dogs exhibit certain behaviors in order to make up for their size. These include barking and general aggression towards other dogs. This description also refers to the fact that some small dogs have obedience problems.

While to some this observation may seem like fact, it doesn't really have much to do with the genetic makeup of the dog. There are big dogs that yap and disobey commands and small dogs that are very docile and polite.

Perhaps this phenomenon can be explained by how owners work with their dogs. In one study, researchers found that small dogs were not as well-behaved as their larger counterparts, but found that this had to do with their owners. In the study, the owners of the smaller dogs used more punishments while training and were less consistent with training.

Photo Courtesy of Sarah Schwartz

As the owner of a small dog, you must consider how you treat your little guy in comparison to your big dogs. If you scoop up and protect your small dog at the first sign of trouble, your dog may believe that there is more to be fearful of than it previously thought. Or maybe you decide not to worry about your Miniature Dachshund jumping on people because it's not big enough to harm anyone. These habits create the perception that small dogs have a certain attitude problem, when the issue really lies with the owner!

Dogs are able to pick up on human cues and use them to shape their understanding of different situations. That, plus leniency when it comes to obedience training, can lead to behavioral issues in your pet.

Fighting Between Your Dogs

Fighting should never be tolerated between dogs because it can cause serious psychological and physical harm. Fighting is not the same as playing or mouthing because the end goal in a fight is to injure the other dog seriously enough to eliminate the threat. Fighting can place a lot of strain on your household, so it's important to understand why fights happen and how to stop them.

When dogs become aggressive, it's because they are afraid. When the stress hormones kick in, their bodies are telling them to run and hide or fight back against whatever is scaring them. When one dog feels threatened by the other, its instinct is to fight. A good way to prevent fights is to notice when your dog is becoming fearful and get it away from the situation.

If a puppy bites another dog, it doesn't mean it's trying to cause pain. Because dogs don't have hands to grab things, they use their mouths. Puppies are still learning how to play with others, so sometimes they accidentally bite a little too hard. Other dogs will correct them and they learn that their little teeth can hurt sometimes. If your dogs are mouthing at each other, but are showing playful body language, they're probably just having a good time.

When a dog shows a sign of aggression like bared teeth, growling, a tense body, or excessive panting, that's a warning sign that something has gone wrong. Calmly and carefully move your dog to a safe place.

If your dog begins to fight, resist the urge to panic. It's a scary situation, but if your dog senses your fear, its own fear will go into overdrive. Firmly call your dog and carefully pull it away if it does not respond.

It's possible that a dog may accidentally bite its owner in this situation because it might not have any idea that the owner is grabbing it and not another dog. If your dog cannot be pulled by a leash or harness, try picking it up by the back legs like a wheelbarrow and drag it backwards until it is out of harm's way. This motion should be swift, as you don't want the dog to focus its aggression on you.

Once the fight has diffused, try to prevent similar issues from arising again. Maybe one dog got possessive over a toy, which caused the fight to break out. Assess the situation and work with your dogs to keep them calm and happy.

Raising Multiple Puppies from the Same Litter

Sometimes, people like to purchase two puppies from the same litter. While this has advantages in terms of introductions, there are also some possible drawbacks. When you bring home two Miniature Dachshunds from the same litter and you don't have any other pets, you can feel confident that the dogs won't have many issues sharing a home, as they are already used to it. While they might look the same, they probably have different personalities and different needs.

Sometimes, dogs from the same litter can develop behavioral problems as a result of never being separated from their sibling. If they ever need to be separated--for veterinary care, for instance--it can cause severe separation anxiety.

Before bringing home multiple dogs, consider the time and effort it takes to raise just one puppy. Puppies are an incredible amount of work. Sometimes, dog owners find that the work involved with multiple dogs is just too much to handle, requiring them to rehome one of the pups. If this happens, they may both experience separation anxiety.

If you're confident in your ability to take care of two individual puppies, then the more, the merrier! Perhaps you have a lot of help at home or have a lot of experience raising puppies. If you're new to dog ownership, think about the kind of commitment you're making when you bring two puppies into your home. You may decide it's easier for you to raise one to adulthood before getting another.

What If My Pets Don't Get Along?

Despite the hours of work and research involved in introducing a new dog, sometimes things just don't work out. If you've tried different approaches and consulted experts and weeks have passed with no improvement, you may have to consider an alternative.

While you can separate your pets for a while, this may not be a great permanent solution. If one pet is really bothered by the presence of another, just its scent may trigger anxiety. As hard as it is to give a pet up, you might have to in order to keep the other ones safe.

Because of this, find a breeder or a dog shelter that allows you to take a dog home for a trial period. It can be tough to figure out if your pets will get along after just one or two meetings, though you might be able to get an idea of how they will act around each other.

Sometimes, the solution is simple. Maybe your pets just need more space and time apart. You can walk your dogs separately so they feel like they have special one-on-one time with you. Maybe your dogs are fighting over food, and two separate dishes will do the trick. There are so many things that can cause disagreements between pets, so do your best to observe tiny behavioral issues.

If you've tried everything you can think of and it's not working out, talk to a professional. A breeder, veterinarian, or dog behavior specialist may be able to offer fresh insight and advice into helping your pets get along.

A Miniature Dachshund can be a great addition to your pet family, but keep in mind that it's not always a smooth transition. You may find that your pets aren't agreeable at first, but give them a little time. Introduce them slowly and allow them plenty of space to meet the other pet. Be aware of the signs of stress and aggression so everyone remains safe. If you run into issues that are beyond your ability to deal with, consult with the experts. They'll help you figure out a plan that is best for everyone.

CHAPTER 9
Training Your Miniature Dachshund

"Dachshunds were bred to be determined, which shows up in them through their stubbornness. This can make training frustrating at times."

Roberta LaCosse
www.havendachs.weebly.com

Often times, owners don't place a lot of stress on obedience training once their dogs have mastered basic housetraining. Obedience training is time consuming, potentially frustrating, and requires a basic understanding of psychological concepts. But when obedience training isn't done, dogs become restless and bored, and will behave in ways the owner doesn't like. It isn't the dogs' fault—after all, they won't know any better unless they're taught. Start early, and you'll find that obedience training doesn't have to be a constant battle with your pup.

This chapter doesn't cover instructions on how to teach commands, but rather the theory and practice behind dog training. The next chapter will feature ideas of commands to teach your dog and details on how to teach each command.

Setting Clear Expectations

Just like when you set house rules with your dog, training requires a clear idea of what your expectations are. For example, if you are leash training your dog and it pulls on the leash a little, you need to decide if you're going to allow it to pull, or if you need it to stay close to your side. If you don't want it to pull, then when you practice, it needs to be corrected each time it gets ahead of you. It makes for a few weeks of tedious walks, but it will lessen your dog's confusion if you keep the training consistent.

When other people in your household are planning on having a hand in your Mini Dachshund's training, it's good to talk about how you plan on training your dog. If everyone uses different techniques, then your dog may become confused. For example, if you ignore your dog when it displays attention-seeking behavior but your partner yells at it, your dog is getting mixed messages. A discussion on how you plan to train your

Photo Courtesy of
Ewa Kasyan

dog will keep everyone on the same page and can even open up discussions about solving your dog's training struggles.

Also, this is a good time to set training expectations for yourself. Before you even start, decide how much time you can spend working with your dog. Especially at the beginning, you'll want to work with your dog for at least an hour a day. Expect to practice with your dog for months, depending on how quickly it picks things up. If you expect your Miniature Dachshund to pick up new commands in a matter of days and perform them under any circumstance, you're going to become disappointed and discouraged. Training can be slow going, so be patient and try to have fun.

A Primer on Operant Conditioning

When training a dog, you need to know a little dog psychology to understand how your pup thinks. While there are many schools of thought on the best way to train a dog, most trainers and owners base their methods on the psychology of operant conditioning.

This type of conditioning is all about how animals respond to the outcomes of certain behaviors. A classic example of this theory in action is an experiment done with rats. A rat in a box with no other variables or distractions has the choice of pressing one of two levers. The lever on the left, when pressed, results in food being dropped into the cage. This is a reward. When the lever on the right is pressed, it results in a painful electric shock. The shock is a punishment. Over time, through trial and error, the rat will learn to only press the left lever, while avoiding the right one at all costs. This is because its brain has been conditioned through reward and punishment to choose the behavior with the desirable outcome.

Parents often use the same sort of conditioning with children, because like dogs, you can't always reason with them. When toilet training children, some parents will give their child a treat for using the toilet successfully. If the child has an accident, no reward is given. The treat is the incentive to use the toilet, as the child's parent wants. With enough practice, the child will continue to use the toilet, whether a treat is involved or not. Even if the child doesn't fully understand why it's important to use the toilet, he or she can understand that the reward is good.

With dogs, you want to make connections between desired actions that they do normally and rewards from you. The goal is to pair a short command with the action that will prompt them to do it, and then give the reward. Over time, they'll learn that if they do the action that goes with the command, they will get a treat. With enough practice, they will follow the command, treat or no treat.

Within operant conditioning, punishments can also be used to shape behavior. However, it doesn't always produce the desired results. Dogs can be so averse to punishments that they will replace one bad behavior with another in an attempt to avoid punishment. Also, if your dog is afraid of you, it will have a harder time learning good behaviors. For this reason, it is best to avoid any kind of punishment system in dog training.

Operant conditioning is different from classical conditioning. With classical conditioning, animals unconsciously respond to a stimulus. Like Pavlov's dogs that salivated when they heard a bell, this type of conditioning doesn't involve making a conscious choice. It can be paired with operant conditioning if you involve the use of a clicker tool. When training your dog, you want it to make the choice to follow your command because the reward is greater than acting of its own accord.

Photo Courtesy of
Emma Massey

Primary Reinforcement

When it comes to types of rewards, there is primary reinforcement and also secondary reinforcement. Primary reinforcement covers rewards that are valuable in and of themselves. These types of rewards are very enticing for dogs because they have immediate value to a dog.

Food is a popular reward for dogs because you'll find that they'll do just about anything for a tasty snack. Dog treats or human foods like fruits or vegetables are exciting to a dog because it's not their usual fare.

When your dog behaves in a way that you want it to behave, immediately give the treat. This will provide instant gratification for your dog. With enough tries, it'll figure out that listening to you results in happiness in the form of a snack.

Dog treats are not the only kind of primary reinforcement that rewards dogs for good behavior. If your dog has a favorite toy and is strongly motivated to listen in order to get that toy, it's a good alternative to a ton of treats. For example, if your stubborn dog doesn't want to come inside after being let out, you may choose to stand at the door with its favorite squeaky toy in plain sight. When it obeys the "come" command, it is rewarded with the toy.

Along with toys, playtime can also be valuable to a dog. If your stubborn Miniature Dachshund successfully uses the bathroom, you may reward it with tossing a ball to chase. That way, it has an incentive to use the bathroom immediately when it goes outside because it knows that something good happens next.

You may feel like giving your dog a treat every single time it follows a command is excessive and will cause weight gain. Some owners also worry that they will have to carry treats wherever they go for the rest of their dog's life in order for them to listen. This is where a variable reinforcement schedule comes in handy.

A variable reinforcement schedule deals with the frequency of your dog being rewarded for good behavior. This means that instead of giving your dog a treat every time, you give treats out randomly. For example, if you command your dog to sit five times, you might give a reward three out of five times. It's a good way to wean it off of constant treats and may be even more reinforcing than giving a treat every time.

One way to think of variable reinforcement schedules is to compare them to a slot machine. People can sit at slot machines for hours, even if they don't win money every time. But one win with a reward of money can entice gamblers to continue to pull the lever, because they know that it's possible they'll win big again. They don't see the reward every time, but they believe after enough pulls, they'll get their reward.

The same goes for dogs and their treats. They'll keep sitting when you tell them to because they know that they've been rewarded for it before, so they may be rewarded for it again.

Secondary Reinforcement

Secondary reinforcement is different than primary reinforcement because these rewards are not valuable in and of themselves, but can be traded for something that is valuable.

The best example of this in the human world is money. Money is really only fancy pieces of paper, but humans have assigned value to it. We then use the pieces of paper to trade in for things that are rewarding in themselves, like food and clothing.

You probably won't be able to convince your dog to lie down for a dollar, so there are different secondary reinforcements that owners can use to motivate their dogs.

In a way, giving your dog praise for successfully completing a command can be seen as a form of secondary reinforcement. When you tell your Miniature Dachshund it's a good doggy for sitting on command, you're telling it words that it doesn't completely understand, because it cannot speak human language. But because owners generally pair verbal praise with belly rubs and happiness, your dog understands that whenever it hears those words, it knows it is loved.

Another underrated training tool that can be used as secondary reinforcement is a clicker. This is a small plastic tool that can be held in your hand whenever you're working with your dog. With the push of a button, a click sound notifies your dog that it is doing exactly what you want it to do.

Because the clicking sound doesn't initially have any meaning to your dog, you will first have to teach your dog to associate the sound with rewards. Giving treats and praise when it hears the clicker helps it realize over time that clicks are good.

Once the clicker becomes a reward, it's time to put it into action. The reason the clicker is so helpful in training dogs is because it's more precise than handing out treats. For example, if you have a particularly active Miniature Dachshund, it might be hard for it to learn the "stay" command because it's wiggling all over the place. If it manages to stay for a few seconds, but run towards you before you have a chance to reward it, then it's hard for the dog to know which behavior you're rewarding.

But with a clicker, you can click after just a few seconds before the dog bolts away. It allows greater precision with rewards, helping your dog learn faster because you can hand out more rewards with greater accuracy. It's also helpful to have a reward system that doesn't involve too many treats, because it's too easy for Dachshunds to pack on the pounds.

Dangers of Punishment

Because positive reinforcement is part of operant conditioning, that means that punishment is too. However, your dog is not a rat in a cage. Therefore, it's best not to teach your dog using fear or pain.

Punishment is different from a negative reward. With punishments, you're giving your dog something that it does not want, like a swat on the nose. With negative rewards, you're taking away something your dog wants.

There are some cases where negative rewards may be appropriate. For instance, if a dog loves to stare out the window, it might bark at people passing by. Of course, this can get irritating quickly, so the owner might want to put a stop to that. The owner may try a negative reward to keep the dog from barking at people by moving the dog into a room without windows that look out into the street. With repetition, the dog may realize that if it barks while looking out the window, it won't be allowed to look out the window anymore.

Punishments, on the other hand, teach dogs to be afraid of their owners. As discussed in the chapter on socialization, dogs react differently to fear. If your Miniature Dachshund is stressed enough, it could become aggressive, or it may cower in fear or hide whenever you are present.

Also, it's hard to predict how a dog will react to punishments as opposed to positive reinforcement. With positive reinforcement, you'll find that your dog wants to do its job in order to get a reward, whatever that may be. With punishments, your dog will do whatever it takes to not receive the punishment, which isn't always the same thing as what you want it to do. For instance, if you spank your dog for chewing on your shoes, it doesn't necessarily teach it that chewing on shoes is bad. Instead, it may find a secret spot to chew your shoes so it can't get caught.

Instead of using anger to deter your dog from unwanted behavior, it's better to catch its attention and divert it to a more appropriate behavior. Dealing with unwanted behaviors will be covered in more detail in later chapters.

Professional Dog Training

Sometimes, a trainer can help a new owner or a particularly stubborn dog. Training a dog is a big undertaking and it's good to find help if it's too much to handle on your own.

There are a few different routes to take with hiring professional help. Perhaps the most popular is to take a class. These are conducted by an experienced dog trainer and have different levels of difficulty. Once your dog graduates from the most basic class, you can find a more advanced class to refine its skills and teach it new things.

Group classes will have different owners and dogs of different breeds present. Not only is this an economical choice, it also allows your dog to socialize with others. If you can teach your dog to stay while eight other dogs are nearby, then you'll have a much better chance of getting your dog to listen to you in other distracting scenarios.

Photo Courtesy of Clara Roberts

Another option is to take a private class. These are able to cater to your busy schedule because the trainer only needs to make plans with one owner. These classes cost more than group classes, but it might be worth it if there's something preventing you and your dog from taking a group class. For instance, if your dog has issues with other dogs, you might not want to bring it to a group class until it's had some initial training.

Finally, you may even choose to send your dog to a trainer that doesn't allow owners to be present. This allows professionals to work one on one with your dog without your dog needing to navigate the relationship with the owner while learning new skills. However, it doesn't always allow owners to work on valuable training skills to continue working with their dog. Unless you're training your Miniature Dachshund to do a very specific job, like hunting, this type of training might not be practical.

If you have others in your household, bring them along to training if your trainer allows it. Not only do classes teach your dog valuable skills, but people can learn a lot from a dog trainer. When your dog practices commands with other family members, it gets a chance to trust and respect all of its owners.

Owner Behavior

Photo Courtesy of Vanessa Higgins

While dog behavior is always discussed when it comes to training, owner behavior should be addressed as well. For a new dog owner, it can be hard to know what to expect when bringing home a new dog. All dogs are different, so the calm, docile pup you imagined may turn out to be a stubborn ball of energy. If the owners don't know what they may encounter with raising a dog, it can be stressful. For this reason, it's important to have an open mind about your new dog and be flexible so you can solve any problems you may face.

Dogs have the ability to pick up on the owner's emotions through voice and body language. Your dog can tell the difference between when you're happy versus when you're angry. Some dogs are particularly in tune with their owner's emotions, and can even manipulate them into getting their own way.

For example, if your dog barks constantly when it's put in its pen, it may find that this irritates you. When it manages to break you down enough, you'll give in to its wishes. If you are patient enough to ignore the barking, it will eventually stop because there is no payoff.

When possible, show your dog happiness when it's behaving, and a firm calmness when it isn't. It is a good idea to practice ways to calm your temper when your dog acts up because the stress isn't good for you or your dog.

While you will probably find that owning a dog is a great joy in life, you'll also discover that you'll feel your fair share of frustrations. This is completely normal. It's especially challenging at first, but you'll find that with a ton of patience and practice, your dog will figure out what you expect.

Miniature Dachshunds are known for being stubborn, so the right owners for these dogs need to be calm, but firm. They can't let their dog control them and plenty of patience is required.

Once you get into the training routine, you'll never want to stop teaching your dog new tricks. When training a dog, make sure to keep things positive for best results. It may take a little trial and error to find what motivates your dog, but once you do, keep working at it. If you find that training is too much to do on your own, find a professional that can help teach both you and your pup.

CHAPTER 10
Basic Commands

"The biggest mistake people make is not starting to train them as soon as they get them."

Lori Noland
www.drycreekminidachshunds.com

Once you understand the basics behind dog training, it's time to start teaching and practicing commands. Miniature Dachshunds are intelligent dogs, so if you can get them in the right mind frame to learn, there's no telling what they can accomplish in a training session.

Benefits of Obedience Training

There are so many reasons why it's important to train your dog. Well-trained dogs are safer and more entertained than dogs that haven't been trained. Not only does obedience training make life better for the dog, it makes life easier for the owner, too. If you aren't completely sold on starting a training regimen with your dog, here are a few reasons why you should teach and practice commands with your dog.

First, teaching your dog certain commands can keep it safe. While tasks like being able to sit and stay are important, your dog will get a lot more out of being able to listen to you. Dogs don't always understand the world like humans do, so they may unknowingly wander into dangerous situations. Miniature Dachshunds are tough and smart, but they need a little extra guidance from their humans.

For example, if your dog manages to slip outside when you open the door, you want to be able to get your dog to stop and come back with a simple command. Dogs don't know that they can be injured if they run off, so it's the owner's job to teach them how to be safe. If your dog can listen to you, no matter how tempting the alternative is, it will be much safer.

Training is also good for your dog's mental capacity and it fights boredom. Dogs (especially ones that were historically bred to work) like to have a job. While you don't necessarily have to teach your dog to hunt for small animals like Miniature Dachshunds used to do, they sometimes need training in order for them to feel like they are working.

Photo Courtesy of
Carmina Morreale

If dogs don't have a "job" to do, they will often make up their own. Miniature Dachshunds, in particular, are wont to dig holes in the ground. If you don't want your dog to create its own destructive jobs, then it's best to give it some replacements. Teaching your pup to fetch and drop an object can make it feel like it's working, plus it'll get good exercise without destroying your yard.

Finally, a well-trained dog makes an owner's life easier. It's much easier to correct unwanted behavior if you and your dog speak the same language. For instance, if you don't like how your dog gets too excited when the doorbell rings, it's helpful to be able to tell your dog to sit and not ambush your visitor.

It's a pleasure to spend time with well-trained dogs because they are easy to control when they get over-excited. They'll be happy because they like learning new things, and you'll be happy because they're on their best behavior. It takes time to get them to the point where they listen to every command, but with practice and good training techniques, you'll get there.

Photo Courtesy of Hayley Whytock

Basic Commands

There are a few commands that trainers teach new dog owners when they are just starting out because they are simple and useful to learn. This section includes some commands that you'll absolutely want to teach your new Miniature Dachshund.

When starting out, find a place to practice that is relatively free of distractions. Once your dog begins to master the commands, practice in places with more distractions. When your dog can listen in a crowded dog park, you'll know that it's got the command down pat.

Sit

This is probably the first thing you want to teach your dog. The "sit" command can keep your dog still and calm when you most need it to be. When it sits, it should stay in the seated position until you give another command. You'll find that your dog is ready to listen for the next command in that position.

To teach the "sit" command, take a treat and raise it just above the dog's head. When its head goes up, its bottom should go down into the seated position. If it has a hard time figuring this out, you may also want to place a hand on its bottom and gently apply pressure downward to let it know what you want it to do. Give the command, and then give the reward once your dog is seated.

Lie Down

"Lie down" is perhaps the next thing you'll want to teach after "sit" is mastered. This next command is good for keeping your dog still and under control. This position takes more effort for your dog to get out of than a sitting position so it's good to use when you need your Miniature Dachshund to stay still for a little longer.

To begin this command, have your dog start in a seated position. Hold the dog treat in front of your dog's nose and slowly move your hand to the ground. As your hand goes down, so should its head. Once it gets into the correct position, praise it and give it the treat. If the dog stands up to get the treat, try holding the treat closer to its body. If you lure it too far forward, it may crawl forward to get the treat. If you are clicker training your dog, you can click before your wiggly dog moves out of position.

Think about the command you'd like to use for this action. Some people say "down" for this position, but it can be confusing if you also plan on using "down" when you want your dog to stop jumping on people or objects. "Lie down" is a good choice because it's different enough from "down".

Stay

Once your dog is in a prone position, it may need to be instructed to stay still until given further instructions. While you may eventually teach your dog that "sit" and "lie down" also include staying still until you give a new command, the "stay" command is a good way to practice being still. This command is useful for keeping an active dog under control.

To teach this command, start with telling your dog to sit or lie down. Once it's in position, give the "stay" command while holding your hand like a stop sign in front of its nose. If it can hold the position for a few seconds, give a reward. Over time, practice holding the position for longer intervals of time. At first, stay close to your dog, but then slowly add distance between you and your dog to make things more challenging. The real test is practicing this command in a stimulating place where there are lots of distractions and things to investigate.

Come

This command can also keep your dog safe from potentially dangerous situations. If you see your active dog running away from you to go exploring, it's important to be able to bring it back with a command. Miniature Dachshunds have little legs, but they can take off pretty quickly. When you call your dog, act excited when it comes to you. If you call your dog in anger because you're about to punish it, it will be afraid come to you and won't feel like it's being rewarded.

When starting out, it helps to keep your dog on a leash and have it sit and stay. Walk to the end of the leash and call the dog to come. Your voice should be inviting and positive, but not too high-pitched and frenzied. If your dog does not come to you, gently tug on the leash to give it a clue about what you want it to do. Once it comes to you, give a reward. When your dog starts to figure it out, add more distance. Once it has this command down, your dog should immediately come to you, regardless of the situation.

Off

An excited Miniature Dachshund pup will likely want to jump up on people and things. While this might seem cute at first, after a while it can be irritating. This command requires consistency among people interacting with your dog. Some may see it as a sign of affection from the dog and want to encourage it, but it can be really annoying for others. If you decide you don't want to allow your dog to jump on people, make it a household rule and stick to it. This is an attention-seeking behavior, so the key is to make sure you don't give the dog what it wants.

To teach this, you'll just have to wait for your dog to naturally jump up so you can give the command. Young pups will probably be eager to jump on new visitors, so before long, you'll be able to anticipate your Miniature Dachshund's next move.

When your dog jumps up, turn your back to show that you are ignoring it and you aren't going to give it any attention when it acts that way. Give the "off" command. When it gets down, give a treat or praise. Another method is to keep the leash connected at a time when your dog is likely to jump. Place your foot on the leash, making it impossible to jump up. When the dog follows your command, reward it.

Drop It

This command can be helpful if you have a curious Miniature Dachshund that likes to claim your objects as its own. It can also save your dog's life if you catch it sniffing something dangerous. For instance, if you catch your dog picking up a dead animal on the street, you need a quick and simple way to keep it from eating the dead animal.

To teach the "drop it" command, give your dog its favorite toy to play with. Next, hold a dog treat in front of your dog's face and give the "drop it" command. Your dog will probably be more interested in the treat than the toy, so it will drop the toy in exchange for the treat. Once the dog drops the toy, give the treat. As your dog becomes better at this command, let it practice in a place with more distractions.

Walk

Leash training is a vital part of the training process. When you take your dog out on a walk, you don't want it to pull on the leash. For its safety and your sanity, you'll want your dog to be right next to you. Your dog should stay close to you with its head in line with your leg. If it bounds ahead or lags behind, it needs to be corrected.

This can take a lot of practice, since many dogs get excited and like to run ahead and pull on the leash. If your dog has never been on a leash, it probably won't have any idea what to do. Bring some treats along with you on a walk, and practice giving the "walk" command and having your dog walk with you. Hold the leash somewhat close, but keep the leash lax. Shorter leashes work better than retractable ones for training.

Start off by slowly walking a few steps together, then stop and command your dog to sit. Once you can get it to walk a few steps beside you before sitting, then extend the number of steps you take. After enough stop and go, your dog will learn that it is supposed to stay near. Whatever you do, don't allow your dog to pull you. If it tries, turn around and walk in the other direction, or stop and ignore it until it comes back and stops pulling.

Advanced Commands

Once you master these basic commands, it's time to challenge your Miniature Dachshund with new commands. If your dog has something new to learn, it's more likely to feel entertained enough to stay out of trouble. Many advanced commands just build on basic commands, so it's not as challenging as you may think. Here are a few ideas of commands to teach your Miniature Dachshund once the basics are covered.

Fetch

This trick will make playtime more fun and challenging for your Miniature Dachshund. Your pup will think it has a job, which stimulates the mind and makes it happy. If it gets good enough at this game, you might even name its toys and have it fetch different objects.

For this command, find a quiet place to practice. Throw a toy to get your dog to chase after it and pick it up. It might not understand that dropping the toy allows you to throw it again, so you can give the command to drop it. If it drops the toy at your feet, give a reward. Then the game can begin again.

Take It

If your dog has mastered the "drop it" command, the next step is to teach it to pick something up. This command can be used for a variety of purposes, from starting a game of fetch to teaching your dog to put its toys away.

To start, place your dog's favorite toy in front of it. Give the "take it" command and wait for it to naturally pick up the toy. When it succeeds, give a treat. Once your dog masters "take it" and "drop it" try introducing the names of its toys or other household objects. Eventually, it may even be able to bring you an object by name.

Go To

This command builds on the knowledge of the names of places your dog needs to go. This can be a helpful command if you need your dog to go to a certain place. For example, you could command: "go to backyard" or "go to crate" to get your dog to go to a safe place. You might also try "go to bed" at the end of the day, or "go to potty".

While there are different ways to teach this command, the simplest one is to start with your dog seated in front of you. Give the "go to place" command and with a treat in hand, lure it to the place. Once it is seated or lying down in the place, give the treat. Once your dog knows the names of the places, you will no longer need to have it follow you there, because it will have made the name association. If it can make it to the place on its own, follow it and reward it with treats.

Training your new Miniature Dachshund can be a lot of work, but once you get going, you'll want to teach your dog everything it can learn. Obedience training is an important part of your dog's development because it gives the skills it needs to live in your home and it keeps the dog entertained. Miniature Dachshunds are intelligent dogs that can be stubborn at times. With a little insistence, this breed can be put to work to do any number of tasks. Just because these dogs are little doesn't mean that they can't do a lot.

CHAPTER 11
Dealing with Unwanted Behaviors

"Do not let you dachshund jump down. Jumping down can jar the spine."

Reba Mandrell
www.heartlanddachshunds.com

Up to this point in the book, we've discussed different ways to help your dog become the best behaved dog it can be! A new owner may expect their new dog to be a blank slate which they will teach all new behaviors, but this is not typically the case. Miniature Dachshunds are known for having spirited personalities; so don't be surprised if they try to make their own rules. This chapter will briefly discuss the less-favorable behaviors we see in dogs, and how to correct them.

What is Bad Behavior?

In dogs, unwanted behaviors are usually classified as anything that is dangerous, destructive, or just plain annoying to an owner. The definition of "bad" behavior is somewhat relative to the owner, because different owners have different standards when it comes to their dogs.

Before you bring your dog home, think about which behaviors you are willing to allow in your Miniature Dachshund and which ones will not be tolerated. For example, virtually all dog owners can agree that biting is a behavior that should never be tolerated. But there are other behaviors, like sitting on furniture, that are annoying to some people and not to others. It's easier to take a hard stance and stick to it immediately after your dog comes home than to observe the behavior and decide afterwards whether you can let it slide or not.

With Miniature Dachshunds, it's likely you'll see some destructive tendencies at one point or another. These dogs are natural diggers, so any opportunity they get to sink their feet into the earth, they'll probably try to burrow. This breed also has a fairly high prey drive, so if they find something that resembles prey, they might try to tear it to shreds. While this can be confined to toys, your throw pillows might not be safe.

Other unwanted behaviors can be dangerous to your dog or to others. Biting and other aggressive behaviors can be dangerous for others, making it difficult to allow anyone near your dog. Aggression towards other dogs can put both your dog and other dogs at a substantial risk if the behavior is not dealt with.

Other behaviors, like escaping and running off, can put your dog at risk for getting lost or injured while navigating the streets on its own. This can also be a sign that your dog does not listen to calls to stay or come.

Finally, there are behaviors that won't necessarily cause serious harm to anyone, but can strain a good relationship between owner and pet. Barking, jumping, whining, and other behaviors may seem inherently harmless, but over time can really grate on an owner's nerves. These types of behaviors also need correction before you become too frustrated to be able to properly handle it.

Finding the Root of the Problem

Just like with training, correcting unwanted behaviors requires you to think like a dog. Your Miniature Dachshund doesn't share your psychology, so you must think on dog terms to figure out what's going on.

As smart as your pup may seem, when it acts, it's reacting to the surrounding environment. While the destruction can sometimes appear to be premeditated, it's usually not that complicated. Dogs think one second and do the next.

In order to correct bad behavior, it's important to figure out what's causing it. Many behaviors have an underlying cause, and if that isn't changed, it can be hard to change the behavior. Whether the issues are caused by a biological need, fear, lack of attention, or are prompted by owners, look to the root of the problem in order to work out the best solution.

With Miniature Dachshunds, many behaviors are ingrained in their DNA, whether you want them to have those behaviors or not. Digging, chewing, and barking are all common issues in Miniature Dachshunds that come from their historical background. These behaviors can be corrected, but it's best to give your dog a more productive outlet for its energy.

Other bad behaviors come up because your dog doesn't feel like it's getting enough attention. Barking, whining, and jumping can all be ploys to get your attention. With these types of issues, your dog needs to learn that bad behavior will not win any attention. When your dog acts up to get your attention, you must ignore it until it stops. When your dog is being good, reward it with praise and playtime. In the meantime, make sure you give plenty of exercise and affection when your dog is being good so it doesn't feel like it needs to beg for attention.

Fear is another reason why dogs might act up. Because Miniature Dachshunds are seldom shy, serious fear can manifest in aggression. Growling, snapping, biting, and fighting can all result from fear. Because this behavior can be seriously dangerous, it's best to leave it to the experts if it gets out of hand. In the meantime, observe your dog and see if you can spot any stressors. Fear is often a result of poor socialization. Another underlying cause of snapping is pain. If you find that your dog growls or snaps at you when you touch it in a certain way, it might be experiencing pain. A dog that comes from a good breeder should not be naturally aggressive, so the owner must figure out what is causing the stress.

Finally, a lot of poor behavior can be attributed to boredom. If your dog gets bored, it will find something to entertain itself. Unfortunately, what it finds will often be destructive. Chewing is common in bored dogs because they need an outlet for all of their mental energy. If they don't have the correct outlet for it, then they will chew whatever they can find. If your dog appears to be acting out of boredom, see if you can increase its daily exercise, add more playtime to your routine, or increase obedience training practices. These are all good ways to stimulate your dog's brain, which can help keep it out of trouble, especially when it is not being supervised.

Dogs' actions happen for a specific reason, whatever that may be. If you can think like a dog and put yourself into their position, it's easier to figure out what needs to change to stop that behavior. With enough work, virtually all behaviors can be changed to be more compatible with your home.

Bad Behavior Prevention

While some behaviors just come naturally to some dogs, others are learned in response to their environment. In order to keep unwanted behaviors at bay, there are a few things you can try to keep your dog from forming bad habits in the first place.

First, make sure your Miniature Dachshund is getting enough exercise, mentally and physically. Your little one needs to go on at least one decent walk a day. Because they're so little, this doesn't have to be a three mile walk, just enough to keep energy levels manageable.

In between walks, play games with your dog to keep its mind active. Fetch is a good game for Miniature Dachshunds because it doesn't require them to jump or be super fast. Tug of war is also a game that your Miniature Dachshund will love. Some dogs can get overexcited with this one, though, so make sure you always initiate the tugging with an appropriate toy and that your dog is able to drop the toy with a single command.

Chew toys, like bones, are also good for keeping your dog busy and out of trouble. Dogs need objects to chew on to satisfy their urge to chew. By keeping a supply of safe, acceptable toys for them to chew, you'll help prevent them from making their own chew toys.

Also, make sure your dog has enough human interaction during the day. Dogs can get lonely, which leads to more boredom. If you are not able to spend time with your dog during the day, and it's causing the dog to act out, you may want to consider hiring a dog sitter or dog walker to check up on it and give your pup a little extra attention.

Another good way to prevent unwanted behaviors around other people and dogs is to work on socializing your Miniature Dachshund. Some behaviors like barking, jumping, and aggressive tendencies can be traced back to the fact that a dog is not comfortable being around strangers. Once the dog has the experience and realizes that there's nothing to be afraid of or over-excited about, some of these behaviors can be easily changed with a little practice.

While these are not immediate solutions to your dog's issues, these are all good things to try if you want to keep your well-behaved dog from picking up any bad habits, or if you're just starting to notice some unwanted behaviors forming.

How to Correct Your Dog

Photo Courtesy of Lisa Korab

Now that you've decided which behaviors you will not tolerate, it's time to teach your dog to avoid them. When teaching your dog not to do certain behaviors, remember that the aim is to correct, not punish. Correction helps your dog change unwanted behavior to acceptable behaviors. Punishment may act like a deterrent in some cases, but it can also lead to more stress for your dog.

When correcting your dog, remember that dogs do not have the mental capacity to remember mistakes that they've made prior to your correction. For example, if you come home after work and find that your dog has used the bathroom in the middle of your kitchen floor, your teaching moment has passed. Even if the dog can see and smell the accident while you're correcting it, it just can't understand the link between those two things.

That's why it's so important to pay close attention to your dog, especially in the early stages. If you catch it in the act of misbehaving, you have the chance to correct the behavior.

When you see your dog doing something you don't want it to do, there are a few ways to correct the behavior. One is to make a sound or a command that lets the dog know that you don't like what it's doing. If you see your dog scratching at your door, clap, or say "no". You can also give a command like "lie down" at this time to get it into a position that isn't compatible with the naughty behavior.

Another way to correct attention-seeking behaviors is to ignore it altogether. When your dog barks non-stop or jumps on you, it's looking for a reaction. Yelling at the barking, while not always positive for your dog, is a form of attention. Turning your back may be enough to signal that you will not participate until it is quiet.

When you make a noise to correct your dog, make it firm and attention-grabbing, but not mean and scary. You just need something to make your dog realize that you know what it's doing. That way, you can try to divert its attention to something else that can be rewarded.

Fixing Bad Habits

Especially if your Miniature Dachshund came from another home, it may have picked up some bad habits that you're now left to deal with. If this is the case for your pup, don't worry! Mini Dachshunds are smart and are capable of learning new behaviors. This will take a lot of work though, because your Dachshund is probably pretty comfortable with its routine and in no hurry to change.

Once you know how to go about correcting bad behavior, you have to be firm and unyielding. Every time you see the unwanted behavior, you must correct it. If you or another member of your household allow the behavior sometimes and not others, the corrections will not stick.

Also, make sure that your own habits aren't encouraging your dog's behavior. If you are annoyed about how your dog begs and whines during your meal, maybe it's because you've been giving it table scraps after supper and it wants the scraps sooner. Perhaps you yell at your dog every time it barks, and it feels like you're joining in with the noisemaking instead of asking it to stop. Take a look at your own behaviors around your dog if you find that you're having a hard time breaking its bad habits.

When to Seek Help

Photo Courtesy of Jessica LeFanu

It can be really challenging to correct unwanted behaviors in Miniature Dachshunds. They are confident dogs that will do what they please if their behavior goes unchecked. While lot of work can be done in the home, sometimes you need a little extra help.

If your dog's behavior is downright dangerous to yourself or others, seek help from a veterinarian or behavioral specialist. They may have a better idea about how to solve your problem quickly, because they've experienced it before. Stressful situations are not always easily avoided, so this type of behavior needs to be addressed immediately.

Also, if you find yourself becoming extremely frustrated or upset by your dog's unwillingness to change, don't feel like you're all alone in caring for your pet. Professional trainers can offer a different perspective and tips that you may not have thought of. They can also observe how you react to your dog, and offer insight into what you can do better when training your dog. It's not good to have an unhealthy relationship between owner and pet because this can lead to more problems in the long run. If you're feeling especially stressed, your dog may sense that.

Even if you're not in a dangerous situation or at the end of your rope, it can be good to get help from a professional before things develop. Every dog is different, and it helps to seek the advice of someone who's seen a lot of different behaviors. A good vet or dog trainer can be an excellent resource for all things regarding your dog.

Unwanted behaviors in your Miniature Dachshund can cause a lot of stress and strain on your relationship with your dog. When you encounter a problem, try to figure out what your dog is looking to achieve with the behavior. Once you know what it wants, channel that energy into something more productive. It takes a lot of time and patience to break bad habits in stubborn dogs, but it's worth it when your dog is able to behave like a member of the family.

CHAPTER 12

Traveling with Miniature Dachshunds

Once you bring your dog home, you'll never want to be away from it again. Luckily, this dog is so small that traveling doesn't have to be a big production. Your pocket-sized pal will be able to fit into just about any mode of transportation you'll have to take. However, traveling isn't always fun or easy for dogs, so this chapter will cover ways to make sure your Miniature Dachshund is safe and happy during your travels.

Your dog will need to ride in a vehicle at one point or another for visiting the vet or going to the dog park, so you'll want to do everything you can to make it as smooth of a ride as possible for your dog. If car rides are a source of anxiety for your pooch, it can make it nearly impossible to get it into the car, let alone expect it to sit still for a ride. Plus, all of that stress isn't good for your pet and can make adjusting to the destination harder.

Just like with any other new adventure your Miniature Dachshund goes on, you'll want to gradually build up exposure to riding in cars until you're certain your dog can handle it.

Dog Carriers and Restraints

If you're driving with your dog in your car, it's extremely important to have a way to keep the dog safe. Most owners wouldn't let their children ride in a car without a seatbelt, yet dogs are not always restrained when traveling. For your pet's safety, as well as your own, it's necessary to have a way to restrain your dog in the car.

There are different ways you can keep your dog from wandering around the vehicle. One of the easiest methods is to use a crate. If your dog is already crate trained, then it will naturally feel a little safer in the crate while riding in a car. The crate is heavy enough that it won't go flying around with every turn and can be restrained even more securely.

This is also a good option for dogs that suffer from car sickness because the sides can be covered to prevent them looking out the window. If your dog cannot see where it is going, it might not feel as queasy on a car ride.

Harnesses are also good for car travel. Special seatbelt harnesses can be fastened to your car's seatbelt, keeping the dog sitting securely in the back seat. Not only will it prevent the dog running around the car, but also keep it from becoming a projectile in the event of an accident.

Because this breed is so tiny, there are also booster seat versions available so your pup can see out the window. Some dogs like the feeling of the wind in their fur, so this allows them to check out the action. Of course, try not to let your dog's head go outside of the window because its eyes can be injured by debris in the air.

Whatever method you choose, make sure it's appropriate for your small dog's size. A crate for a Golden Retriever is too spacious for your Miniature Dachshund, and a harness that is too big can be slipped out of easily. Just like you would with a child, fit your dog for a safety restraint before your first car ride together. In the event of a crash, you want to make sure your pup is securely fastened.

Getting Your Dog Ready for Rides

Photo Courtesy of Des Goaten

Some dogs just hop in the car and are ready to go. Others are hesitant or even terrified to travel in a car. If your Miniature Dachshund is part of the latter group, then you'll have to do a little work to get it ready for car trips.

To start out, get your dog used to the feeling of sitting in a motionless car, fastened in with your restraint of choice. Let your dog sit in the car for a while and see how it reacts. Once it becomes calm, reward it.

The next step is to drive a short distance. If your dog is really nervous, you don't want to make this ride too long. A few trips around the block will do. Once you let your dog out of the car, reward it with treats and praise. The goal is to make a connection between a car ride and a reward. Make this as positive as possible.

Once your dog starts to feel comfortable with short trips, take it on slightly longer rides. You can go to a park across town or to a friend's house. Wherever you go, make sure the experience is positive and that your dog gets a reward for riding in the car.

If your dog doesn't like car rides because it gets motion sickness, try to restrict its view of the road while in the car. A crate or dog carrier can make it harder for it to watch objects rush by the window. If that doesn't help, you may want to talk to your veterinarian about medications that can help with nausea. If car rides are unavoidable for your carsick pup, you'll want something to ease its upset stomach.

Before going on a long car ride, make sure your dog has time to stretch its legs and use the bathroom. Once you're on the road, try to make stops every couple of hours to let the dog relieve itself and get a little exercise. You don't want a hyperactive dog restrained for too long, or else it'll try to keep itself entertained in a way you might not like.

Flying With Your Miniature Dachshund

Car rides can be hard enough on your dog, so just imagine how potentially stressful a flight can be. But if you need to take your dog somewhere and driving isn't an option, you might have to take your dog on an airplane.

Luckily, this breed is so small that you can probably keep your dog with you in the cabin. This is a better alternative than putting it in cargo storage because you can ensure that it's doing okay and feeling calm. However, airlines have strict rules about what is allowed as far as bringing a dog aboard goes. If you don't buy an extra seat for your dog, then it will have to be stowed in a carrier that can fit below the seat.

Before you bring your dog on the airplane, make sure it has a chance to go to the bathroom. If possible, try to make sure it gets a little exercise before you get on the plane. The last thing you want is for your dog to start barking up a storm in the middle of the flight because it's bored and restless. With any luck, it'll be exhausted enough to take a little nap during the flight.

Regardless of whether your dog's carrier will be kept in the cabin or in the cargo hold, make sure it is clearly marked with all of your contact information in case it gets lost. Also, make sure your dog has enough water and food if the flight is going to be long. If your dog will need to use the bathroom during the flight, tuck a few potty pads inside the carrier for easier cleanup.

Before travel, do thorough research on your airline's policies about dogs. Different airlines have different rules and you don't want to learn an unexpected piece of information regarding your dog when you're trying to get on a plane. Also, make sure your dog is up to date on its shots, especially if you are entering a different country. Dog owners must respect the laws put in place by other countries to prevent the spread of disease to their animals.

Hotel Stays

When booking a place to stay during your trip, make sure your hotel accommodates dogs. You don't want to face large fines from your hotel or be asked to leave because you didn't do your research. If possible, choose a hotel with a green space for your dog to walk and go to the bathroom, or see if you can book a place with a nearby park.

While you're out and about, try to bring your dog with you whenever possible. Most dogs don't like to be kept alone in a small room all day, and especially not when it's an unfamiliar place. If your dog is crate trained, it may feel a little more secure, but at some point, it's going to need attention from its owner.

Make sure you bring all of the comforts of home for your dog while staying in a new place. A familiar blanket will keep it comfortable, while its favorite toys can keep it entertained. Make time in your schedule for plenty of exercise, because a destructive dog can cost you a lot of money in your rented hotel room.

Kennels and Dog Sitters

Photo Courtesy of Vince DiGuglielmo

If you cannot bring your dog on your trip, or you know that you can't give it the attention it needs, your other option is to find someone else to care for your dog. Both dog kennels and dog sitters are options that have different pros and cons.

A dog kennel is like a little hotel for dogs. While not all kennels are fancy, they provide a small, contained space for your dog to hang out while you're gone. With a kennel, you have different employees who are responsible for making sure your dog is doing fine without you. Many kennels are fairly affordable because there are several customers in their care at once.

A good kennel will give your dog plenty of exercise and attention, while allowing your dog to play with other dogs. There should be employees present for most of the day, so there's always someone nearby when your dog needs them. If your dog is well socialized with other dogs, it may love being able to play with so many different dogs.

If you take your dog to a kennel, make sure it is up to date on shots. If possible, visit the kennel and look for reviews before booking your dog's stay. Look for nice, clean facilities and kind, knowledgeable employees. It makes going on a trip much easier if you know you can trust the people looking after your dog.

A dog sitter is another good option when you must leave your dog home alone. This is best if your dog is wary around other dogs or has separation anxiety. This allows your dog to remain in your home while someone makes frequent visits or stays in your home with your dog.

While in-home sitters may cost you a lot more than a dog walker, they provide a better level of care for needy dogs because they always stay with the dog, even at night. An added bonus is that you can have someone watching your home if they're staying over.

During the process of hiring a sitter, bring the sitter to your home to meet your dog. You should be able to tell if the sitter is a good fit for your dog and knowledgeable about Dachshunds. You want to choose someone both you and your dog like.

Because you know your Miniature Dachshund well, you'll be able to decide which care option is better for you and your pup. While kennels are more affordable and allow your dog to socialize, a dog sitter might be better for dogs who need the comforts of home. Choose someone you trust, because it will make your time away much easier if you know your dog is in good hands

Tips and Tricks for Traveling with Your Dog

When traveling with your dog, there are a few things you can do to prepare your dog for a ride. First, make sure your dog's exercise, food, and bathroom needs are met before you get into the car. You don't want to have to pull over or clean up a mess an hour into your trip. If you plan on leaving around your dog's usual meal time, try to feed it a little earlier than usual. If your dog experiences car sickness, a meal given immediately before the trip could reappear on your leather seats. Good exercise before a trip can keep your dog tired while you drive, causing the both of you less stress from an energetic dog that has nowhere to release its energy.

Make a checklist of your dog's necessary items before you go. For long trips, make sure you have a leash for rest stops. Even if your dog does well walking off the leash, it can be spooked or excited by a new

Photo Courtesy of
Joanne Atkinson

place and run off. Its collar should have your contact information on it in case the worst happens.

If your dog gets nervous, it can help to have an extra person sitting in the backseat with your dog. Soft, soothing voices let your pup know that it's going to be okay. Try not to get your dog too riled up with excited, high-pitched voices. You want your dog to be calm and relaxed during your ride.

Your dog should have plenty of access to clean water on your trip. You'll also need food if you're planning on being away during the next meal. Bring plenty of treats, especially if your dog is not a fan of riding in the car. Toys can make your dog's ride better if it gets bored easily. A favorite squeaky toy can be comforting, and a good chew toy can keep your dog busy for hours.

When going to a new place, keep in mind that it can be an exciting and potentially scary time for your dog. In order to keep it happy, try to give it as many familiar items as possible. Try to keep to your regular daily schedule, and when all else fails, reassure your dog and give it plenty of treats. With enough preparation and practice, hitting the road doesn't have to be a bad experience.

CHAPTER 13
Nutrition

W hat your puppy eats can help determine how healthy it will be as an adult. Good food, exercise, and genetics shape a lot of your dog's overall health. But there are so many foods on the market to choose from that it can be a daunting task to figure out what to give your dog for meals. A basic understanding of what nutrients your dog needs and how many calories it should ingest will help you figure out what's best for your dog. This chapter will explain the specific kind of nutrition Miniature Dachshunds need.

The Importance of a Good Diet

Photo Courtesy of Ewa Kasyan

While all dog food may seem like the same smelly, crunchy brown kibble, there's a lot that goes into it. Your dog needs the right balance of carbohydrates, protein, and fats, not to mention all the vitamins and minerals. Because your dog is eating one kind of food for every meal, you'll want to make sure the food has everything it needs.

Miniature Dachshunds are genetically predisposed to have certain health conditions. While big dogs might need more carbs for energy, little dogs need more protein to keep their muscles healthy. If your dog doesn't get the right nutrition for its unique body, it may face health conditions in the future.

Nutrient deficiencies can lead to problems with major organs and the skeletal system. This breed is prone to spine problems so if they don't get enough vitamins and minerals, it can affect how their bones grow. Obesity is another common problem in this breed and it's mostly due to food intake. Too much food or the wrong kinds of foods can make your dog overweight, putting a lot of unnecessary strain on its body.

Even within the breed, every dog is different. Some dogs can eat certain foods with no problem, but others have gastric distress from specific ingredients. As an owner, you must observe your dog's signals that something is making it feel ill so you can find a solution. Just like humans, some dogs have food allergies and intolerances that can make them feel sick.

Essential Nutrients for Miniature Dachshunds

Dog food should have plenty of protein—around 20 percent of their diet. Dogs also need small amounts of fat for energy, brain health, and to keep a shiny coat. Look for a dog food with about 5 percent fat for adults, and a little more for puppies. Omega-3 and Omega-6 fatty acids are best because they help with brain function to keep your Miniature Dachshund sharp. Lean proteins like fish and poultry provide plenty of protein, while staying light on fats. For dogs that aren't very active, look for a dog food that is light on carbohydrates. If they're not using the extra energy from the carbs, then it could cause them to gain weight.

When it comes to carbs, some might work better with your dog's system than others. Whole grains like oatmeal, brown rice, and barley are good for dogs because they take more time to digest. This means that the energy is released more slowly, keeping your dog feeling energized all day. Simple carbohydrates like white rice are easy to digest, which is easier on sensitive tummies, but it only gives short bursts of energy, requiring more food to make your dog feel full and energized all day. Complex carbs also have more fiber, which keeps your dog from getting too hungry before the next meal.

Some owners don't like to give their dogs foods that contain grains like corn, wheat, or soy because of the way certain dogs digest these grains. Some dogs have sensitivities to these ingredients, which can cause digestive problems. However, if your dog can digest these grains with no problem, you probably don't need to completely avoid them. There are, however, more nutritious carbohydrate sources that can give your dog good, long-lasting energy.

Your little dog needs a lot of protein to keep its strong muscles healthy. When it comes to meats, each different type of animal tissue provides different nutrients that are good for dogs. Poultry and fish are lean and contain good fats for your dog's coat. Red meats like bison, lamb, and beef provide iron, which is necessary for blood cells. When you feed your dog foods that have different types of meat, there's a better chance that your dog is getting all of the nutrients it needs from its protein source.

While some dog food companies use whole meats, a lot include an ingredient called meal. Meals, like chicken meal, also contain organs, bone, and cartilage. While this can sound kind of gross, it provides dogs with a good source of nutrients. Bones, organs, and cartilage all contain nutrients that are excellent for bone and joint health, which is important for Miniature Dachshunds.

You'll also want to make sure that your dog has enough fat in its diet. Dogs need animal fats to keep their coats healthy and shiny, and to break down fat-soluble vitamins. Fats also provide long lasting energy for your dog and can help it feel full. Without good levels of fats, your dog's fur will look brittle and dry.

A dog food that contains calcium and glucosamine can help with bone and joint problems. Most dog foods that contain fish or leafy green vegetables will naturally have calcium to keep bones from becoming brittle. Glucosamine may be added to foods as a supplement for joint health. These supplements, which are often added to dog foods, can keep your dog youthful and active into old age.

Fruits and vegetables are often overlooked in your dog's diet, but they're a good, natural way of making sure your dog gets the vitamins and minerals it needs. When looking at the list of ingredients in your dog's food, check if there are a wide variety of colors in the produce. The more colors you see, the wider the range of nutrients. Real fruits and vegetables also provide fiber without adding a lot of calories.

Mini Dachshunds have a long lifespan compared to other breeds, and a good, nutritious diet can give them a better quality of life in their old age. Good fats, lean protein, and vitamins and minerals from vegetables will help with maintaining a healthy weight, skeletal health, brain health, and good vision. Skeletal conditions can leave your dog in a lot of pain, but a healthy diet can help prevent these issues.

Different Types of Dog Foods

Photo Courtesy of Kathryn Thomas

With so many dog foods on the market, it can be hard to choose just one. When picking out a dog food, you'll want to compare ingredients, formula, and price.

When given the choice between wet and dry food, consider your dog's needs. Wet food is good for dogs that have mouth and tooth problems that keep them from being able to eat crunchy food. However, in healthy Miniature Dachshunds, dry food can help keep their teeth healthy.

When a dog eats crunchy food, the hard, scratchy surface of the kibble scrapes against the teeth, taking plaque with it. As your dog chews, it works like a little toothbrush, cleaning the gunk off of the surface of the teeth.

With wet foods, the meaty bits stick to the teeth, making it easier for plaque to form and stick onto the teeth. If it isn't scraped off, either with crunchy treats or a toothbrush, it can lead to tooth decay.

Wet foods can be helpful if your dog is especially picky and refuses to eat dry food. The water in wet food helps it give off a strong aroma, which is enticing for picky dogs. However, it's not great for your dog's teeth in the long run. If your dog refuses to eat dry food, you can give your dog a mixture of wet and dry food. Or you can add a little broth to the top of the dry food, helping release the good smells. Over time, change the ratio of the mixture until it's eating the dry food without any problems.

If your dog struggles to eat crunchy kibble, look at the size of the bits. If it's eating a large dog formula, the pieces of food might be too big for its little mouth. Miniature Dachshunds have small, pointed mouths, so a small kibble is easier for them to chew. You may even want to try a dog food with different shaped kibble.

You'll also find that there is a wide range when it comes to price. Luckily, this breed doesn't eat as much as larger breeds, so it's a little more affordable to splurge on a more expensive brand. However, there are some mid-range brands that are perfectly fine. Just look at the label when you buy food to make sure the ingredients used will give your dog excellent nutrition.

Homemade Dog Foods

An alternative to commercial dog food is homemade food. Homemade foods are good for dogs that have allergies or intolerances to certain ingredients. These diets are also popular amongst owners who are careful about feeding their family raw or unprocessed foods, and want to do the same for their pets. However, when done incorrectly, it can lead to serious nutrient deficiencies.

Dogs need meat, so any efforts to feed a dog a vegan diet would be irresponsible. Dog food recipes should always be double-checked by a veterinarian and followed carefully without making any substitutions. When done correctly, homemade dog foods can be very nutritious and tasty for your dog.

Making your own dog food can be time-consuming and expensive. The reason that dog food companies can produce so much food for such a low cost is because they get their ingredients in bulk and often use the cheaper cuts of meat. Also, where their ingredients fail to deliver necessary nutrients, a vitamin supplement is added to cover it. Some owners, though, just don't like the idea of feeding their dog ingredients that they would not eat themselves. When it comes to homemade dog foods, remember they are only healthy for your dog if they include everything your Miniature Dachshund needs.

Feeding Your Dog People Food

After a meal, many owners share their scraps with their dog. It cuts down on food waste, and the dog seems to enjoy it. However, food scraps can be dangerous to dogs, especially breeds like Dachshunds.

Miniature Dachshunds tend to gain excess weight easily, and people food can contribute to that. When feeding instructions are followed, your dog should get all the calories it needs from its dog food. Anything extra that cannot be burned off will be stored as fat, and gaining weight can cause strain on the body.

Also, dogs aren't used to eating the same types of foods as humans. Certain ingredients, like onions, are found in a lot of people foods, but are harmful for dogs. Artificial colors and flavors may not affect your body, but can make your dog ill.

Not only are table scraps not very healthy, they can also reinforce annoying begging if you feed your dog straight from the table. This can cause your pup to whine during your meals if left unchecked. If you cannot resist sharing your leftovers, make sure you give it to your dog well after your meal, in a location away from the kitchen table.

This doesn't mean that all of our foods are bad for dogs. Fruits and vegetables can be a healthy part of your dog's diet. Berries, leafy greens, and steamed sweet potatoes are all very nutritious and can be used as training treats. These foods are low in calories and can give your dog an extra boost.

Weight Management

While chubby pups can look adorable, extra weight can really wreak havoc on your dog's health. Dachshunds have long spines that are susceptible to injury if there is too much pressure in the wrong places. This breed gains weight fairly easily, so it's important for owners of Miniature Dachshunds to keep a close eye on their weight.

One way that Miniature Dachshunds gain weight is from overeating. If you aren't sure how much your dog should be eating, check the dog food bag. There should be feeding guidelines that use your dog's weight to calculate how much food it should get per day. Different dog foods have different calorie counts, so start with what the bag suggests and then adjust for your dog's needs. For instance, if your dog is young and particularly active, then it can eat a little more than a senior dog that isn't getting as much exercise.

If you aren't able to weigh your dog to make sure it's not getting too chubby, look at its body shape. From above, your little sausage dog shouldn't look like a sausage. There should be a clear waistline between its shoulders and hips. You should be able to feel the ribs easily with light pressure, but not be able to see them.

If you find that your dog is overweight, try adjusting its calorie intake and exercise output. Make these changes slowly so you don't overwork your dog. If the weight problem persists, talk to your vet about finding a different dog food that will help it lose the extra pounds.

Your dog's diet is important to its overall health. The right nutrients can fuel your active, feisty dog. On the other hand, the wrong foods can make your dog feel ill or can make it feel tired or cranky. When choosing a dog food, don't be fooled by the claims made by dog food companies. Read the ingredients in the dog food to ensure your pup is getting everything it needs in the right amounts.

Photo Courtesy of Laura Scott

CHAPTER 14
Grooming Your Miniature Dachshund

"Dachshunds are a medium shedder. All dogs shed to some extent. They should blow their coat once a year. If they are shedding a lot it would indicate a health problem. Groom your dachshund on a regular basis which will vary depending on which coat type you have."

Reba Mandrell
www.heartlanddachshunds.com

Miniature Dachshunds can have different kinds of coats, so their grooming needs may differ depending on their coat type. A lot of your dog's grooming can be done in your home, but there are some tasks you might want to save for a groomer. This chapter will cover all of your Miniature Dachshund's grooming needs and how to meet those needs. With a little work, you'll have your dog looking nice and feeling confident in no time.

Coat Care

Photo Courtesy of Sarah Schwartz

If your Miniature Dachshund has a short, smooth coat, then your work is fairly simple. These dogs just need a good brushing once or twice a week. Brushing helps remove hairs that your dog has shed along with dirt and debris picked up from playing outside. A thorough brushing with a soft bristled brush can also help distribute the natural oils in your dog's coat, helping it to look clean and shiny.

Because these types of coats don't grow to be very long, they don't require any trimming. Give these dogs a good brushing a few times a week, and they're good to go!

Long-haired Miniature Dachshunds require a little more work with their coats. Because it can get tangled so easily, the coat needs to be brushed several times a week. Otherwise, the fur can become matted, which can be painful for your dog. A pin brush can help keep the top layers tangle free and a slicker brush can get below the surface to remove loose fur and prevent mats.

If your long-haired Dachshund's fur gets too long, it can be hard to keep clean and tangle-free. You may decide to take your dog to a groomer to help brush out mats and trim up its long fur. While it is possible to trim your dog's fur at home, groomers are trained to safely use scissors and other trimming equipment around dogs. Also, they have a lot of experience and a good eye for how your dog's coat should look.

If your dog's coat looks dry and brittle, then there's something wrong. First, check if you're using any products on your dog that may be keeping it from looking glossy and shiny. Over-shampooing your dog can strip natural oils from the coat. If that's not the issue, then maybe it isn't getting enough fats and oils in its diet. You can supplement a deficiency with fish oil supplements. A dry coat can also be a symptom of a few different medical conditions, so if you can't fix the problem yourself, talk to a vet for more testing.

Bathing

Unless your Miniature Dachshund is very dirty and smelly, try not to bathe it too often. Shampooing too frequently can strip the fur and skin of the natural oils that keep them healthy. Aim to bathe your pup once every few months, unless it gets itself into a mess. Some dogs don't like bath time, so you'll want to do your best to make it a positive experience. Speak to your dog in a soothing voice, and try not to panic if your dog doesn't immediately comply. This will only get it riled up.

First, make sure the water temperature in your tub is not too hot or too cold. It helps to have a detachable shower nozzle for rinsing your dog. Otherwise, a cup filled with tap water will do. Don't dump water on your dog without letting it feel the water first. A bunch of too-hot or too-cold water all at once is a good way to give your dog a bath aversion. Once it's comfortable with the water, get its entire body wet, excluding the face and head.

If your Miniature Dachshund has a long coat, you'll definitely want to make sure you brush out all the tangles before a bath. Once wet, the fur is much harder to brush, making matting worse. Plus, you'll get the added benefit of having less fur to clean out of the drain if you can remove some of it before your dog hops into the tub.

Next, use a little bit of shampoo to work the fur into a lather. Dogs often have skin allergies that act up when they get in contact with certain chemicals, so choose a gentle shampoo that's free of extra perfumes or dyes. Once its body is all soapy, use the shower nozzle or cup to rinse your dog off, starting at the top and working your way down. When you think all of the soap is gone, rinse again. If shampoo is left on the skin and fur, it can leave a buildup that can cause itchiness in your dog.

It's best if you save the head and face for last. Pouring water and scrubbing with shampoo in your dog's face makes it harder to keep soap out of the eyes, ears, nose and mouth, leaving you with one unhappy dog. Instead, use a moist washcloth to wipe these areas.

Once you take your dog out of the tub, pat it dry with a towel. If your Miniature Dachshund gets cold and shivery easily, you might want to dry it with a hairdryer set on the lowest setting. Otherwise, your dog will be able to air dry just by shaking off and running around your home.

Once your dog is completely dry, give it a good brushing. This will fix any remaining tangles. Wet fur stretches and breaks when you brush it, so make sure you wait until your furry friend has had enough time to dry off.

When bath time is all over, give your dog a treat. This will help it associate bath time with tasty goodies. Your dog may test your limits during a bath, but if you stay calm, it will be more likely to stay calm too.

Trimming Nails

Trimming your dog's nails is an often overlooked grooming task. While some owners leave that work to the professionals, it's fairly simple to do at home, too. Frequent nail trimmings are good for your dog's feet because when the nails get too long, it puts too much pressure on the feet when the dog walks. Also, when you keep your dog's nails trimmed, the blood supply to the nail, or the quick, doesn't grow as far down. That means there will be less pain for your dog if you trim frequently.

Plus, if your dog doesn't have long, sharp talons, it is less likely to scratch you or your furniture.

Before you get out the clippers, get your dog used to having its feet and toes touched. If your dog can't handle that, then trimming its nails will be a struggle. Touch the feet and toenails when your dog is sitting still. When you're done, give a reward. Once it's fine with having the nails touched, then you can trim them.

When trimming the nail, position the clipper so the pointed nail will be trimmed into a flatter surface. You should trim enough of the nail that it no longer touches the ground. If you aren't sure where the quick is, trim little by little. You don't want your dog to associate this time with pain. If you do hit the blood supply, you can dip the nail in clotting powder or cornstarch to stop the bleeding.

Once all of the nails are finished, reward your dog. If you find that your dog is wiggling away after a few nails are finished, maybe give it a break and do the rest at a later time. Because of the risk of causing your dog pain if you cut too far, it can make a lot of owners nervous. If you aren't sure, you can always ask the vet to show you how at a checkup. Or you can leave that work to your vet or groomer for a small fee.

Brushing Your Dog's Teeth

Oral hygiene is extremely important for dogs. Not only do sore, decaying teeth make it harder to eat, but the bacteria from dirty teeth can travel through the bloodstream and create problems in the internal organs. It seems trivial, but good oral hygiene can really extend the life of your dog.

Just like with nail trimming, your dog will not enjoy having its teeth brushed if it isn't used to having its mouth and teeth touched. Before you introduce the toothbrush, work on gently pulling the lips back to expose the teeth and lightly touch each tooth. Reward your dog after it sits still for a practice session.

There are different products on the market made for your dog's teeth. There are special toothpastes that use enzymes to clean your dog's teeth. These do not have foaming agents or fluoride like human toothpaste, because your dog needs to be able to swallow it. They are usually flavored with dog-friendly tastes like poultry or peanut butter. Special dog toothbrushes are small enough to fit your dog's mouth. There are even brushes you can slip on the end of your finger for ease of brushing.

Before you brush for the first time, let your dog lick a little of the toothpaste from your finger. If it tastes good enough, your dog might think having its teeth brushed is a treat. Then gently brush the outside surface of their teeth. If it's too hard to reach the other surfaces, that's okay. Crunchy kibble will help scrape the inside surfaces of the teeth.

Cleaning the Eyes and Ears

Photo Courtesy of Karen Hitchman

Eyes and ears are sensitive areas, so a gentle touch is required. A dog's eyes tend to tear up and leave goopy residue below the eyes. A little bit of this is natural and can be gently wiped away with a damp cloth. If the eyes are leaking a lot of discharge, they may be infected and a veterinarian can prescribe something to help them. Try to avoid any cleansers that aren't made especially for a dog's eye area. When bathing, don't shampoo near the eye area, as it can cause irritation and pain.

Because Miniature Dachshunds have floppy ears, they need to be kept clean and dry. When bathing your dog, you may even want to place cotton balls at the front of the ear openings to keep water out. When water gets trapped, it becomes a perfect breeding ground for bacteria. An ear infection can cause a lot of pain and discomfort for your dog.

If there's a lot of waxy buildup in your dog's ears, there are specialty ear cleaners for dogs that you can purchase from your veterinarian. To clean your dog's ear, squirt a little bit of the solution in the ear and use the outside of the ear to massage it down into the ear canal. Then, using a cotton ball, wipe the moisture and residue from the outer part only. Don't wipe too far down because you may damage your dog's delicate ear.

If you notice that your dog is shaking its head a lot or has abnormal discharge coming from its ear, see your vet. It could be a sign of infection.

Professional Grooming

If you have a long-haired Miniature Dachshund, you may need to take your dog to a groomer to get trimmed up. Regular grooming can keep your dog from becoming matted. Also, if your dog has mats, a groomer has the right tools to get that taken care of. One visit every six weeks or so should keep your dog looking good.

To find a good groomer, talk to your breeder or veterinarian. Your vet's office may even have an in-house groomer. You want to take your dog to someone you can trust to treat your dog well and give it a good cut.

When you arrive at the groomer's for the first time, it may help to bring a picture of what you want your dog to look like. This way, you can't be surprised when you go to pick up your dog and it looks completely different than how you imagined it would look.

Grooming your dog doesn't just make it look beautiful, but also keeps it healthy. Your Miniature Dachshund will be feeling more confident than ever when its fur looks clean and shiny and its teeth sparkle. Start grooming your dog at an early age, and you'll make a difference in how it acts and feels later in life.

Photo Courtesy of
Ian Fletcher

CHAPTER 15
Basic Healthcare

Your Miniature Dachshund's good health is probably at the top of your list of priorities as a pet owner. Whether it's veterinary care or preventative care at home, you want your dog to have the very best. A long, healthy life for your dog is easier to achieve if you are proactive about its care and start while it is young. Diet and hygiene can go a long way for your dog, but there are a few more things to consider when looking at your dog's overall health. This chapter will cover the very basics of your dog's health from the first vet visit to how to keep your pup parasite-free at home.

Visiting the Veterinarian

Going to the vet doesn't have to be a negative experience for you or your Miniature Dachshund. In fact, your veterinarian is an incredible resource for everything you need to know about your dog. If you follow the guidelines in the earlier chapter about picking the right veterinarian, you're well on your way to having a great relationship with your dog's healthcare provider.

If this is your first dog, then you probably have a lot of questions for your vet. Watch as your vet examines your pup and ask about what "normal" looks like in your dog. That way, you can be the first to know if something's not quite right with your Mini Dachshund.

When you arrive, your vet will weigh your dog. Make a mental note of what your dog weighs so you can make sure your dog is a healthy weight between checkups. The vet will let you know whether your dog is within its target weight range for its size.

Next, the vet will have your dog stand on the examination table. This is a great time to utilize your sit, lie down, and stay commands on a squirmy dog. The vet will listen to your dog's heart and lungs, and feel along its body for any unusual lumps or bumps. They will look inside your dog's ears and mouth and at its eyes. If you're nervous about taking care of your dog's ear hygiene, this is a good opportunity to get tips on how to keep ears clean and dry.

Finally, your vet will administer any vaccinations that your dog may need to keep it up to date. When this happens, try to keep your dog calm, but don't make a big deal out of it. If your dog suddenly hears you speak in a high-pitched anxious voice, it will figure something is up and react more to the shot than it would if you kept calm.

Before you bring your dog to the vet, you can practice all the steps that may cause your dog to get stressed out. Practice riding in the car so it has one less thing to worry about. Socializing your dog with other dogs and people can make it less anxious in the waiting room. Finally, practice touching all parts of its body like a veterinarian would. For example, if you can get your dog comfortable with someone touching its teeth, it will be less likely to snap at the vet. After these practice sessions, and the real visit, give your dog a reward. If your dog fights you every time you go to the vet, there's a chance you'll just stop going. Instead, you want your dog to feel safe visiting the vet.

Photo Courtesy of Pauline Goring

Fleas and Ticks

Because your dog will spend some time outside, it needs to be protected from external parasites. Nasty creatures like fleas and ticks can hop on your pet during one of its adventures and eat its blood. This can lead to skin irritation and potential illness in your Miniature Dachshund. Luckily, there are things you can do as an owner to protect your pup at home.

Fleas are so small that you might not even spot them before they multiply. These pests reproduce quickly, so a few fleas turn into an infestation in no time. Their saliva causes a reaction in your dog's skin that makes it very itchy. Not only does the itching feel uncomfortable for your dog, the constant scratching can also break open the skin, leaving it open to infection.

If your dog has fleas, the fleas and their eggs need to be killed immediately. There are special shampoos and combs that can help you remove all of the little pests from your dog's skin and fur. Topical skin treatments and collars also contain chemicals that can kill these parasites. These products need to be used with caution because they can cause illness in pets and children if ingested.

Ticks are much easier to spot because they can swell up to multiple times their original size when engorged with your dog's blood. These bloodsuckers can carry diseases that can be transferred to your dog and make it very sick. If your dog has enough ticks, they can suck out enough blood to cause anemia.

Ticks are usually picked up when your dog runs through tall grass and wooded areas. After a walk in rugged terrain, check your dog's skin for ticks. If you find one, you'll have to remove it immediately. Firmly grasp the tick as close to the head as possible and pull straight away from the skin. Use a firm grip and pull hard enough to get the tick off. This can be harder when the tick is engorged because their bodies can pop with too much squeezing. Once the tick is removed, squash it so it doesn't return to your pet.

There are collars, skin treatments, and oral medications that can keep both ticks and fleas off of your dog. These are good for dogs who spend a lot of time in different outdoor areas. These external parasites are harder to treat when they spread, so try to take care of a pest problem immediately.

Worms

Worms are internal parasites that feed off of your dog from the inside and can make it sick. These are harder to spot than fleas and ticks because the worms often enter the body as eggs and are only found in bowel movements or through veterinary tests.

Most worms take up residence in your dog's digestive tract. Intestinal worms can cause weight loss, diarrhea, intestinal blockage, or vomiting. As with external parasites, if these worms ingest too much of your dog's blood, the dog may become anemic. If you notice a change in your dog's appetite and bowel movements and you're sure food intolerances aren't to blame, it's a good idea to make an appointment with your vet to get things sorted out. A stool sample can help the vet determine which worms are present in order to give your dog the correct treatment.

Because these types of worms spread through fecal matter, it's important to keep your yard especially clean at the first sign of an infestation. It's unpleasant to think about, but some dogs have the bad habit of eating their own (or others') fecal matter. You don't want your dog to re-infect itself after clearing all the worms out.

Heartworm is a dangerous internal parasite that lives within the blood vessels, as opposed to the digestive tract. These eggs enter the body through mosquito bites and can travel through your dog's blood, often ending up in the heart and lungs. These parasites make it harder for your dog's important organs to do their jobs, and if not treated, they can result in death.

Fortunately, there is medication that your dog can take on a monthly basis that can prevent heartworms from surviving in its bloodstream. If your dog is not currently on heartworm medication, your veterinarian will probably take a blood test to ensure it isn't already infected. It's possible for dogs to survive a heartworm infestation, but it takes a lot of expensive care. Remember, it's much cheaper and easier to prevent issues than to treat them.

Supplements and Holistic Healthcare

There are tons of health supplements for dogs on the market that promise all sorts of different benefits, and there are different reasons why dogs might need to have their diets supplemented with different nutrients. If your dog has certain medical conditions that make it difficult for its body to absorb specific nutrients, an added supplement can keep it from having a vitamin or mineral deficiency.

A multivitamin supplement can also help dogs that aren't getting the nutrition they need from their diet. Most commercial dog foods have added supplements to ensure your dog's vitamin and mineral intake is up to vets' standards. But if your dog is eating a homemade diet, a supplement can help keep it healthy.

Before giving your dog extra supplements, talk with your vet to make sure you're giving the right ones. Some vitamins, when taken in excess, can cause more harm than good. Other times, your vet may encourage you to try supplements if your dog has issues with bone and joint health, for example. Just remember, dog supplements aren't regulated by any governing body, and some companies aren't as legitimate as others. A veterinarian can be a good source to help you find out which supplements are helpful and which aren't useful for your dog.

Holistic heath care is an alternative to traditional veterinary medicine. This type of care focuses more on natural remedies to treat illness and injury in dogs as opposed to pharmaceuticals. While it is possible that there are certain plants and herbs that can benefit animals, these treatments aren't usually studied to the extent that commercial drugs are. A vet can help you figure out which remedies have merit and which are pseudoscience. Just because a treatment is natural doesn't mean that it is necessarily safe.

Vaccinations

Starting at a young age, your Miniature Dachshund will need to be regularly vaccinated so your dog and others are safe from disease. Regardless of whether you get your Miniature Dachshund from a breeder or adopt it from a shelter, there's a good chance it's already had a few of its shots.

Some vaccinations are mandatory, while others are not. Vaccinations for parvovirus, distemper, rabies, and hepatitis are necessary for the good health of your dog. Bordatella, Lyme disease, and various respiratory diseases can also be vaccinated against. Depending on where you live, there are laws regarding rabies vaccinations and how often they are required. At the minimum, your dog should be vaccinated for rabies once every three years.

Your veterinarian can help you keep track of when your dog needs boosters on these vaccinations and can help you determine which ones your dog needs. While some owners have their own reasons for not wanting to vaccinate their pets, vaccinations can be very important to your dog's health. Plus, when you vaccinate your dog, you can help stop the spread of diseases between your dog and other animals.

Pet Insurance

Photo Courtesy of Sarah Schwartz

While health insurance is important for people, many pet owners don't realize that pet insurance exists. You may not think you'll need it, but it can be extremely helpful if your dog becomes seriously ill or injured. Routine care is fairly affordable, but the bills can add up fast if your dog needs surgery or treatment. Unfortunately, some owners can't afford expensive vet bills and just choose to euthanize their dog instead of paying the money to treat the issue. If you have pet insurance, you don't have to worry about choosing between your dog's life or spending the money.

Just like with human health insurance, there are some policies that are better than others. Find something that covers your dog's pre-existing health conditions and can cover genetic ailments that are common in Miniature Dachshunds.

If you opt not to buy insurance for your dog, make sure you put some money aside for your dog's healthcare. It can be hard to predict when your dog will need vet care, so make sure it won't send you into financial hardship to take care of your dog. In addition to your funds for yearly checkups, set aside a few extra thousand dollars to make sure you can pay the bill if the time ever comes.

Good healthcare plays a big role in the health and happiness of your Miniature Dachshund. Because your dog can't tell you when it's not feeling well, it's up to you to notice changes in your dog's appearance and behaviors and get the help it needs. There's a lot to think about when it comes to the health of your dog, but luckily, your veterinarian can help you with all of your concerns. Because you love your Miniature Dachshund, you want it to live a long and healthy life, and good healthcare can make that happen.

CHAPTER 16
Advanced Miniature Dachshund Health

"A person considering getting a Miniature Dachshund needs to be aware they can live upwards of 15 years."

Lori Noland
www.drycreekminidachshunds.com

Partially because of how dogs are bred to fit certain standards, certain breeds tend to acquire specific types of injuries and diseases. Good breeding can help lessen the risk of these disorders, but unfortunately, it is difficult to eradicate common genetic disorders in all breeds. Buy from a breeder that does health clearances on their dogs, because that will give you some peace of mind that your puppy isn't at a high risk for developing diseases later in life. If the parents have undergone genetic testing for certain disorders and the tests are all clear, it increases the chance that you'll bring home a healthy pup.

As with any breed, Miniature Dachshunds have their own set of breed-specific health risks that can appear at any point throughout their life. Fortunately, if you know the warning signs, you can get medical intervention that can lessen the severity of these conditions. This chapter will cover illnesses and injuries that are specific to the Miniature Dachshund and ways to help prevent these issues. The list may seem long and scary, but just because it's common in the breed, it doesn't mean that every Miniature Dachshund will see all (or any) of these problems in its lifetime.

Common Genetic Ailments in Miniature Dachshunds

One of the major things you'll want to look out for in your Miniature Dachshund are diseases of the skeletal system. Bone, joint, and disk disorders are all fairly common in this breed, in different forms.

Hip dysplasia is a condition that is common in a lot of different dog breeds. This occurs when your dog's leg bones don't create a perfect fit with the hip joint. When that happens, your dog is at greater risk for injury, just in daily activity. This condition is very painful for dogs, and if it isn't treated, it can lead to lameness of the back legs. Limping, hopping, difficulty standing up from a prone position, and pain with touch are all symptoms of hip dysplasia.

Patellar luxation is a condition that affects the patella, or kneecap. These dogs have little legs, so the shape of their bones and joints comes into play here. With patellar luxation, the kneecap slides in and out of place. This can result in a lot of pain if it happens while your dog is in motion, like running or jumping from a high surface. A lot of times, the kneecap will slide right back into place and your dog will continue to move without excessive pain. Other times, the patella remains dislocated and will need to be put back into place by a veterinarian.

Intervertebral Disk Disease can also affect Miniature Dachshunds because of the unique shape of their bodies. This condition can cause a lot of pain in your dog's back, especially if it is injured. For this reason, it is not good for Miniature Dachshunds to leap from tall heights or be held without proper support. Symptoms of this condition include pain, paralysis, problems moving the back legs, and incontinence. If your dog develops this condition, surgery will be required. This condition can be devastating to an active dog, but proper care can help a lot.

Gastric torsion, or bloat, is a common condition in dogs that have deep chests, like Dachshunds. This condition is related to the way your dog ingests food and water and can become very serious if not treated. When deep-chested dogs eat too much, too quickly, or take part in strenuous exercise after a big meal, their stomach fills up with too much gas and can twist. When this occurs, your dog is not able to release the gas or vomit. If the stomach twists like this, it can cut off blood flow to other parts of the body. Symptoms of this condition include dry heaving, excessive salivation, lethargy, rapid heart rate, and a distended belly. If this issue is not resolved by a veterinarian, the dog can go into shock and even die.

This condition can be prevented by finding ways to slow your dog's eating. There are special bowls that have obstacles in the way, making it harder for your dog to eat fast. You can also try to keep your dog calm for a little bit after meals to give its body time to digest the food.

This breed is also prone to eye and ear conditions that eventually cause blindness and deafness. Retinal atrophy is common in a lot of breeds. This is the slow breakdown of the retina in the eye. When this begins, your dog may only suffer from night blindness, while its day vision is still acceptable. But over time, its vision will deteriorate until it is completely blind. This usually doesn't progress into complete vision loss until later in adulthood. While it can create obstacles for your dog, vision loss progresses slowly enough that there is some time for your dog to adapt to the point that you may not be able to notice a change in its vision.

Deafness isn't nearly as common in this breed, but it is more common in double dappled Dachshunds. This is due to recessive genes from two dappled parents crossing to make a double dappled dog. If you are buying a dappled pup, ask your breeder about its lineage and ask for health clearances related to deafness in the parents.

For unknown reasons, epilepsy pops up more in some breeds than others. Dachshunds are prone to epilepsy, which results in seizures. While seizures can be frightening to both owner and dog, if they are mild enough, it might not result in any long-term issues. Symptoms of epilepsy include seizures, stumbling while walking or running, hiding, and disorientation. If you notice that your dog is having seizures, visit a veterinarian as soon as possible. They can prescribe medication that can lessen the severity and frequency of seizures and give you tips on how to make your dog more comfortable.

Cushing's Disease is a condition where the Dachshund's body produces too much of the cortisol hormone. Cortisol is a stress hormone that can be detrimental to the organs if too much is flowing through your dog's veins. This condition is typically a result of a malfunction in the adrenal or pituitary glands. Symptoms include excessive thirst and excessive urination. A vet can determine how serious the case is and can determine if medication is enough or if surgery to remove a gland is necessary.

Finally, Dachshunds are often at risk for diabetes, mostly due to the fact that they gain weight easily. Diabetes Mellitus is more commonly found in obese dogs. Symptoms include excessive thirst and urination and weight loss despite a normal or above average appetite. If your dog seems to be gobbling up all of its food and still loses weight, or is always thirsty, have your veterinarian test its blood. If the results come back positive for diabetes, you'll need to administer insulin shots to your dog.

Health Risks in Small Dogs

Small dogs tend to live longer than large breeds, but they still come with their own health problems. Because Miniature Dachshunds are bred to be smaller than the average Dachshund, they may be more prone to other health issues. Make sure you buy from a breeder who doesn't try to breed smaller than normal for the Miniature Dachshund standard, because that opens the dogs up for severe, and often times fatal, health problems.

Because your dog's body is so small, it will have a harder time adjusting to the elements than a larger dog with more surface area. This means that both cold and hot weather can be dangerous for a Miniature Dachshund. When walking your dog in the winter, you may want to have it wear a sweater or jacket to help keep it from losing too much body heat. In the summer, keep strenuous exercise to a safe amount when it's sweltering out. Plenty of cool water and shade can also help keep your pup cool.

It may seem obvious when you look at a tiny dog like a Miniature Dachshund, but their skeletal systems are a little more fragile than you'd find in a large dog. A fall or rough handling can really injure your dog. To keep your dog safe, make sure that everyone who handles your dog knows to support its body while holding it, and to be gentle while playing. You don't need to be a hovering doggy parent, but a little extra caution is sometimes necessary.

Photo Courtesy of Jessica LeFanu

Illness and Injury Prevention

Sometimes, despite our best care, our beloved dogs can become ill. Often times, it's an unavoidable part of life. However, there is a lot that dog owners can do to prevent illness and injury in their puppies. If you start good health and hygiene practices early, many genetic conditions can be lessened in severity.

With Miniature Dachshunds, perhaps the number one way to prevent pain and illness is to keep your dog at a healthy weight. Miniature Dachshunds have a higher risk for becoming obese than many other breeds. Obesity can wreak havoc on your dog's body. Even a few extra pounds can put stress on delicate bones and joints. Because this breed already has a lot of risk when it comes to joint disease, too much stress can aggravate these issues.

Also, extra fat collects around internal organs, making them have to work harder in order for your dog to operate at its full capacity. Unfortunately, this extra work can cause the organs to wear out faster. A chubby pup will have a harder time running and playing if its body isn't functioning at maximum efficiency.

A healthy weight can be achieved with the right balance of diet and exercise. If your dog eats a diet of healthy food, but does nothing but lounge around all day, the extra caloric energy will turn into body fat. Similarly, if your dog exercises regularly, but eats whatever it wants, it will gain weight quickly.

Don't feed your dog more than the dog food label says is acceptable for its weight. Feed your dog twice a day and stick to your feeding plan. Free eating, snacking on table scraps, and even too many doggy treats can add way more calories than your dog can burn.

Give your dog exercise in the form of a daily walk and play time. A game like fetch is good for keeping your dog active. Just remember: never push an overweight dog to exercise to the point of exhaustion. If you're trying to get your lazy pup into shape, start slow and gradually work your way up to more exercise.

If you're sticking to the feeding guidelines and giving your dog plenty of exercise and it's still overweight, talk to your vet about changing your dog's diet. They may suggest cutting more calories or even changing the food. If that doesn't work, your vet may even want to run tests on your dog to see if there's an underlying medical reason that your dog can't lose weight.

If your dog is of a healthy weight and still suffers from joint pain, you may want to make sure your dog's daily nutrition includes ingredients like glucosamine and chondroitin sulfate. These are often found in dog food in supplemental form or as chicken meal. These compounds may be able to reduce pain and lessen joint damage in your dog.

In general, a good diet full of vitamins and minerals can support a lot of the body's functions that are affected by these conditions. Antioxidants from fruits and vegetables and Omega fatty acids from fish oil are great for a lot of organs in the body. A healthy dog food can keep your dog's body strong so it will be less susceptible to disease and injury.

Finally, remember to be cautious about your dog's delicate body. Miniature Dachshunds have a unique body shape that can be injured if mishandled. Try not to let them jump from tall furniture and make sure their bottoms are supported when you hold them. Their spine and hind legs can be injured from too much rough play.

It's nerve-wracking to read a list of conditions that are common with your dog's breed, but keep in mind that your dog may never encounter any of these issues. As a dog owner, it's important to know what your dog is like at its healthiest, so you can quickly spot changes. If you suspect your Miniature Dachshund is suffering from any of these common conditions, talk to your vet right away. A speedy diagnosis and quick medical intervention can keep illnesses from progressing and can even save your dog's life in some scenarios. Practice preventative care and don't be afraid to consult a professional if you have any questions.

CHAPTER 17

Life with an Aging Miniature Dachshund

Raising a new puppy through that early stage is a lot of hard work. Once your dog enters adulthood, you'll find that its behavior changes and it becomes a more mature version of its young self. Eventually, it will enter into a new life stage as a senior.

Your aging Miniature Dachshund comes with new requirements to keep it happy and healthy. Your old dog will slow down a little, and its diet, exercise, and hygiene will change to reflect that. This doesn't mean that your fun times with your dog are over. A senior dog is still full of life and brings joy to its owners in new ways.

Basics of Senior Dog Care

Just like when your dog was a puppy, your senior dog will need a different type of care in the latter stage of life. In small dogs, like the Miniature Dachshund, the senior stage starts at around eight years of age. Of course, your Mini Dachshund may live way past that age, but it will probably start to show signs of aging around that time.

If you find that your dog's behavior has changed, this may be in response to aging. Dogs sometimes get a little moodier as they reach senior status. But if you find that your dog just doesn't respond to commands like it used to, there may be something else causing this. Ears and eyes will lose their sharpness with age, so the problem may be that your old dog just can't see or hear you like it used to.

You may have to adapt to your dogs' failing senses. Try not to get frustrated if your dog can't follow your commands. With any luck, it will already be well conditioned to be on its best behavior. Avoid sneaking up on your dog since you may give it a bit of a shock if you approach when it can't hear or see you very well.

It's possible that your dog's patience might decrease a little with age, too. Sometimes, old dogs just don't want to put up with some of the annoyances that they used to tolerate. This means that an elderly Mini Dachshund might get annoyed more easily with noisy children. If your dog is moody or even growls when it gets irritated, give it some extra

Photo Courtesy of
Elaine Brechin

space. But if your dog undergoes a big behavioral transformation, then there may be something more than old age going on.

Physically, your dog will have more aches and pains as it gets old. Dogs can develop arthritis, especially if they've already suffered from joint problems as a young dog. This means that it's just a little harder for them to get up after taking a rest, and they might not be able to walk or run as far as they used to. Expect your dog to slow down a little, but if you can tell it's in serious pain or experiencing lameness, your vet may be able to help with the pain. An extra soft pillow or bed can help your dog feel more comfortable when it rests. If it lets you, you might even try to gently massage sore muscles and joints. The warmth from your hands can help loosen up stiff joints.

Your dog is probably not going to adapt very well to big life changes at this stage, either. Your dog's mind might not be as sharp and it can get confused more easily. Big changes, like a change in caretaker, a change in schedule, or a new home, can throw it for a loop. It's not always possible, but you'll want to try to keep things steady for your dog. For example, if you have to leave for a few days, finding a sitter your dog knows will be easier on it than sending it to a kennel.

Grooming

Even in old age, your dog will feel more confident when it's primped and pampered. But your dog's comfort should never be sacrificed in order to keep up with regular grooming. Because your dog might be sensitive in certain spots, you'll want to be careful not to cause pain. Otherwise, good hygiene is an excellent way to keep your dog healthy.

Gum disease and tooth problems are common in older dogs, so be careful not to use too much pressure when brushing. However, you'll still want to keep up with your dog's oral hygiene because the bacteria that cause gum disease can cause other health problems. If you've brushed your dog's teeth regularly throughout its life, it shouldn't have too much gum bleeding when you brush.

Nail clipping is also very important to keep up with in advanced age. Long nails can put a lot of pressure on different points of the foot. Because older dogs tend to have more aches and pains in their joints, long nails can cause even more pain. Your old dog might not want to sit still for very long, so you might want to trim the nails one paw at a time if your pup isn't receptive to staying put.

If you have a long-haired Mini Dachshund, you'll want to keep up with brushing its fur on a regular basis. Like with other types of grooming, if your dog gets too uncomfortable standing in one position, let it get up and move around. If your dog develops mats, then it will likely have to be shaved, which could be unpleasant for your dog.

When bathing your dog, take extra care to make sure it doesn't slip and slide around. A fall onto a hard surface can cause serious injury at this age. A non-slip mat on the bottom of your bathtub can help keep your dog safe while bathing. Also take extra care to keep your dog dry and warm after bathing because it may have a harder time regulating its body temperature.

When it comes to professional grooming, your groomer should have the knowledge and experience to groom an elderly dog. Older dogs need an extra gentle touch while having their fur brushed and trimmed. The groomer should make sure that your dog cannot slip around on the table, and may even have a padded cushion for it to sit on.

If your dog's age is causing its bottom to be a little dirty after going to the bathroom, you might want to ask your groomer to trim that part a little more to keep the hair out of the way. Trimming that area can help keep your dog (and your home) cleaner, but you might still want to wipe it with a rag when necessary.

*Photo Courtesy of
Kristen Yoh*

Nutrition

As your dog ages, its dietary needs might change a little too. Depending on your dog's activity level, it will probably need fewer calories. As a general rule, the older your dog is, the fewer calories it needs to stay at a healthy weight. If your dog isn't burning as many calories as it is eating, then it will gain weight. Extra weight at this age can make worn out joints even more painful.

There are special dog foods on the market that cater to a senior dog's needs, but you may find that your finicky dog won't be receptive to a sudden change in food. However, there are some nutrients that senior dogs need to feel good, so choose a dog food that contains plenty of what your dog needs.

Fiber is good for making your dog feel full after eating. Because your dog shouldn't eat the same amount as it did when it was three years old, it's good for it to feel full after eating. Plus, a little extra fiber can keep its bowel movements regular. Be advised though, a lot of extra fiber can give your dog gas.

Photo Courtesy of Sue Forrest

As your dog's joints begin to break down, a little extra glucosamine might help slow down the physical signs of aging. A lot of large dog formulas contain cartilage or supplemental glucosamine, but it isn't considered as vital for small dogs. Because Dachshunds have more joint issues than other small dogs due to their body shape, they may benefit from a little extra animal cartilage in their diet.

If your old dog has tooth problems, then eating crunchy kibble can be painful. To soften your dog's hard food, you can pour warm water or soup broth on top of the food. Not only does it make the food easier to chew, but it will smell and taste more appetizing to your dog. If your dog isn't eating crunchy food, keep in mind that food will stick to the teeth more easily. A good brushing in the evening can help clean the wet food off of the teeth.

Exercise

Just because your dog is old, it doesn't mean that you shouldn't give it the exercise it needs. If its body is a little worn down, though, you'll want to be more gentle. For example, instead of running around with your little dog, take it on a slower walk on a soft surface, like grass. If you like to chase your dog around the yard (and your dog still enjoys it), shorten that time incrementally as it ages.

Keep a close eye on your dog at this age. It might follow along even though it's tired. If you notice that your dog is getting tired, give it a rest. You don't want to push too hard. Bring water with you on your walks in case your tired Miniature Dachshund needs to rest its tiny legs.

As long as your dog is able, don't stop giving it exercise just because it's getting up there in age. Daily exercise will keep your dog feeling healthy and entertained. Play isn't only physically stimulating, but also mentally stimulating. Good exercise will help your dog maintain its daily schedule and keep it happy.

Mental Exercise

In addition to physical exercise, your dog needs to exercise its brain, too. You may find that your old dog seems a little confused at times, like its mind's not all there. Some dogs develop dementia when they're old. Dogs with dementia go through behavioral changes and get confused easily.

Good genetics and regular mental stimulation can keep your dog feeling sharp in its old age. Simple things like throwing a ball around for your dog or giving it a chew toy can keep it entertained and can stimulate the mind.

There are even puzzle toys for dogs on the market that are made to keep smart pups busy. These can range from chew toys that have holes to store treats in to plastic puzzles that your dog must manipulate with its mouth and paws to find the treats. These are good toys for young dogs to keep them out of trouble, but also good for old dogs to keep their minds working.

Socializing can also keep your dog entertained at the senior level. If it gets annoyed by other dogs easily, a play date may be a better option than a trip to the dog park. Also, spending time with other people (when your dog is feeling up to it) can help it use the social skills it learned as a puppy. Interacting with others can stimulate parts of the brain that it might not get to use as often as a senior dog.

Senior Health

In addition to the wearing down of the joints, your dog may encounter other health issues that are related to age. Senior dogs are more prone to diseases like cancer, kidney disease, urinary tract infections, heart disease, and liver disease. A lot of diseases can be kept at bay with a good diet, exercise, and general care, but some diseases are just a sign that your dog's body is worn out. This is fairly normal with dogs. It's sad to see your dog's health decline, but it comes with this final stage of life. Veterinary care is still very important, as your vet can help catch these health problems early and make sure your dog gets the care it needs.

Your young Miniature Dachshund might have been able to bounce right back from injury or illness, but it's a bit harder for older dogs. Parasites may not be a big deal to a young dog, but they can take a lot out of an old dog. Skeletal injuries take longer to heal, and cuts and scrapes are easily infected, as your dog's immune system just isn't as strong as it used to be. Injuries will require immediate attention at this age.

While there isn't a lot you can do to ease the aches and pains, try to make your dog as comfortable as possible. Extra padding in its favorite sitting spots can make it feel more comfortable. Even gentle doggy massages can ease joint and muscle pain and make your dog feel loved.

When It's Time To Say Goodbye

As hard as it is, there will come a time where you might have to consider options for the end of your dog's life. Deciding to euthanize your dog is never easy, but it may be a humane way to end your dog's suffering.

There are a few signs that your dog may be ready to go. If your senior dog is depressed, lame or paralyzed, or incontinent, these are all signs that its body is failing. However, putting your dog to sleep should always be a last resort. The vet can advise you on the subject, though they can't make the final decision. When talking to your vet, ask them if there's anything to do to ease your dog's pain and suffering. If there isn't, then you'll have to make the call. It's never easy to lose a pet, but if you can help it pass on without too much suffering, you may be doing your dog a kindness.

Your dog may be getting up there in years, but that doesn't mean that its life is at all close to being over. You and your dog can still take part in all sorts of adventures. It may require a little extra care and caution as it ages, but it's still the same Miniature Dachshund that you know and love.

Miniature Dachshunds are such a fun breed to raise. They have so much personality packed into their tiny bodies. Not only are they adorable and unique, but they are also smart and confident. While they can be stubborn at times, they are incredibly loyal and loving dogs. Once you meet a Miniature Dachshund, you'll want to bring one home.

Caring for a new dog is an incredible amount of work, but it's all worth it when you can spend time with your tiny companion. These dogs will test your patience, but once they're trained, they'll follow you wherever you go. They are capable of doing all sorts of tricks, which will never cease to delight your friends and family.

Being the owner of a Miniature Dachshund, is a big responsibility. You'll find that you'll do anything to make sure your Miniature Dachshund has the best life possible. It's an absolute privilege to bring this breed into your home and have a hand in raising it from a puppy to a senior.

CPSIA information can be obtained
at www.ICGtesting.com
Printed in the USA
LVHW080705170222
711372LV00003B/84

9 781952 069581